Swinging on the
Garden Gate

Swinging on the Garden Gate

A Spiritual Memoir

Elizabeth J. Andrew

SKINNER HOUSE BOOKS / BOSTON

Printed in Canada.

Cover design by Suzanne Morgan.

Front cover photograph by Leonard D. Andrew. Used with permission.

Text design by Terry Bain.

ISBN 1-55896-409-6

Library of Congress Cataloging-in-Publication Data

Andrew, Elizabeth, 1969–
      Swinging on the garden gate : a spiritual memoir / Elizabeth Andrew.
         p. cm.
      ISBN 1-55896-409-6 (alk. paper)
      1. Andrew, Elizabeth, 1969–   2. Spiritual life—Christianity.
   I. Title.

   BR1725.A346 A3 2000
   289.1'092—dc21
   [B]

                                                               00-44578

10 9 8 7 6 5 4 3 2
04 03 02 01

All epigraphs are from *The Secret Garden* by Frances Hodgson Burnett.
New York: HarperCollins, 1987.

We gratefully acknowledge use of the following material:

An adaptation of "The Fear of Growing Things" was previously published
in *Blessed Bi Spirit,* edited by Debra Kolodny. New York: Continuum, 2000.

Meditations With Hildegard of Bingen by Gabriele Uhlein.
Santa Fe, NM: Bear and Co., 1983. Reprinted by permission of the
publisher.

Excerpt from *Present Moment Wonderful Moment: Mindfulness Verses for
Daily Living* (1990) by Thich N'hat Hanh reprinted with permission of
Parallax Press, Berkeley, California.

Scripture taken from the *Holy Bible New International Version®*. NIV®.
Copyright © 1973, 1978, 1984 by International Bible Society. Used by
permission of Zondervan Publishing House. All rights reserved.

Acknowledgments

With profound gratitude, I recognize the following people for their part in the creation of this book: Larry Sutin, Mary Rockcastle, Deborah Keenan and Julie Neraas, all teachers with vast patience, open hearts, and the courage to be honest; my writers' groups, especially Lynne Maker Kuechle, Katherine Barton, and Linda Hennessey, who read so many drafts of this manuscript that we lost count, and Marsha Peck, Carolyn Crooke, and Terri Whitman for helping me with the fine tuning; Joy DeHarpporte, Emily Brown, Rehoboth and our sun-filled days; Lila Parrish for the many free massages; the ARC community for supplying words when I was stuck and for giving me mornings to write; Joan Drury, Marilyn Crawford, Kelly, Norcroft and the Women's Harmony Fund; Mary Benard; Jeanne Audrey Powers for coming to my defense; Marcy and my parents, who caught my exaggerations and filled in the blanks, and who believed this book was possible; Cil Braun for her steady support; and, finally, Jeanne Wirpsa, who set me on this journey so many years ago.

For the people of PPUMC

and for my family

Through animate eyes I divide the seasons of time.
I am aware of what they are.
I am aware of their potential.
With my mouth I kiss my own chosen creation.
I uniquely, lovingly, embrace every image
    I have made out of the earth's clay.
With a fiery spirit I transform it into a body
    to serve all the world.

Hildegard of Bingen

*For you to come out will contribute to the well-being of us
all insofar as you are participating in shaping the Sacred
among us.*

Carter Heyward

Table of Contents

Preface   xiii

Skirting the Garden   1

A Childhood   11

Unlocking the Garden   49

Dormancy   57

Woman in a Wilderness   79

Into the Garden   115

Digging with a Pointed Stick   125

A Queer, Pretty Place   131

The Fear of Growing Things   141

Simon Emanuel   149

Thinking Only of the Magic   163

On Fire   167

Swinging on the Garden Gate   191

Preface

Every story begins with a word: a daunting word, a word that mars the pure white page or inks the air.

A word has upright bones and sinews; it is created the way a body is created—from dirt and spit. It walks about relating to other words until it is a part of an extended thought or metaphor or entire narrative telling how the world began. The world began in chaos, like a rough draft. It began with the faith that creation is good.

Once I carried within me a word so potent that it spread through every artery and vein until my tongue swelled with silence. I carried it into the faculty lounge at a middle school where conversation ranged from marriage to the two-car garage. The word sat rock-hard in my stomach, beside the cafeteria lunch I wolfed down in twenty-two minutes. I carried it with me through the corridors, where one student called another queer and sent me raging, dragging him into the classroom by his shirt sleeve. Angled against the blackboard, arms crossed, he defied me with his eyes. My red-faced fury didn't go far; I forced down the real word and ranted instead about inappropriate behavior and put-downs. I carried it with me through three years of semester reviews with my principal, as we hassled over the inclusive range of paperbacks on my classroom shelves. She was always cordial. The books that passed muster were those that didn't make any waves. Sitting before her wide desk, the boundaries of my body became retaining walls while inside raged the tidal wave of a word.

I carried my word into Sunday worship with a liberal congregation in the heart of Minneapolis. Adult education that morning was a panel discussion on bisexuality; should the church's statement of intentional welcome include bisexuals alongside gays and lesbians? My eyes widened as several people described their experiences of being drawn to both men and women and made a case for celebrating the expansive diversity of God's creation. The word inside me turned restless and eager. I wanted to grow on my spiritual journey—to move forward after years of stasis—and I had a hunch that speaking my word would set me in motion.

I was terrified. Coming out in any form cracks the world open. When we come out, we take a buried truth, an inward reality residing near the soul, and pull it to the surface where it wreaks havoc on every perpetuated falsehood. We yank a piece of our essence out into the air, transforming in the process the self we thought we were as well as the community around us. I came out bisexual, claiming with pride God's presence in the unique desires of my body. But as soon as I could recognize incarnation within my own skin, it was everywhere else as well—in my past, in the landscape, in each object, in the story itself.... The middle school where I taught seventh-grade English couldn't accept my word, but (thank heavens!) my church did, and now the religious contingent marching in the Gay Pride Parade is one person larger. Where the word is spoken, the huge creaking wheels of creation begin to turn.

What stuns me is how the word of God resides in each of us, carved into our very cells. I was taught to look for the word in the Bible, whose onionskin pages seem holier than those of a paperback novel and whose well-worn language we like to associate with the voice of God. After I came out, scripture stumbled down from the pulpit. It never belonged there in the first place: The word became flesh (not with Jesus, who simply reminds us of this fact, but in the very beginning) and it dwells among us, full of grace. When I sink into the sensual and relentless truths of my sexuality, and find there, hidden in the sticky recesses of my sex where I least expect it, holiness, it seems to me that all of creation's bones and blood, vapor, soil, feathers, and solidity are infused with a sacred word. God is thoroughly, unabashedly incarnate. The spiritual journey is so physical that it makes me shiver. It sends me running barefoot on deer-paths through the woods, and it shakes me awake during the blackest part of the night.

There are as many scriptures as there are stories told with integrity. I've found Frances Hodgson Burnett's *The Secret Garden* to be as rich a parable to guide my journey as any told by Jesus. The word of God inhabits our lived stories, the ordinary way our days unfold, and it inhabits the craft by which we give our stories form. What follows is my attempt to recognize that spark of spirit embedded in the solid matter of my life—in childhood, in coming out bisexual, in encounters with death and loss and wild growth—with the hope that my journey might be an invitation for others to do the same. The word comes alive when we claim what is sacred (life-giving, fundamental, charged with mystery and frightfully beautiful) within our stories. This is how we become the word, walking about in the world. We breathe in deeply, down through the lungs and diaphragm to the core, and then release that intimate mingling of air and vibrating flesh into speech. We voice a truth. We create, and in so doing participate in our own creation.

I hunger to hear sacred stories. As a gift to encourage others, I offer my own.

Skirting the Garden

There were walls all around the orchard and trees trained
against them, and there were bare fruit-trees growing in the
winter-browned grass—but there was no green door to be
seen anywhere. Mary looked for it, and yet when she entered
the upper end of the garden she had noticed that the wall did
not seem to end with the orchard, but to extend beyond it as
if it enclosed a place at the other side.

The mixing bowl is half-full with cut broccoli heads. I work
at the stems, slitting the knife under their tough skin, peeling the roughage away, chopping the tender core. The slices
fall from my knife in neat rows of flowerlets. With the dull
back of the blade, I scrape them into the bowl. The rubbery
leaves I heap into the compost bucket.

The kitchen is bustling. This may be a contemplative retreat
center, but today, in the kitchen, you'd hardly know it. Two ket-
tles of soup are on the stove, the pile of dishes beside the sink
is growing unmanageable, and Scott and MaryJo, my community members, dash in and out of the dining room with
tray-loads of dishes. At noon we will feed lunch to over forty
people. Most are seminarians on a silent retreat; from the
kitchen window, I watch them walk past the garden with journals in hand, shuffling through the leaves on the lawn. The

course they are taking is called "Contemplative Living in Modern Society." They have come up from their frenzied academic schedules in the city to sample quiet and perhaps learn what it means to listen. Through the window I watch as one young woman climbs the red oak where the tree swing hangs. I imagine the coarse bark under her embrace and wonder what she is praying for. Another older man heads into the woods barefoot, despite the chill October air. For forty-eight hours, these students will not use their voices and have no scheduled activities other than morning and evening prayer. Outside this kitchen, the house feels as still as the waiting heart of God.

But inside, the knife hits the cutting board with rapid *thwacks.* I've forgotten to take the bread out of the freezer in time to defrost, and so a dozen loaves are lined up for their turn in the microwave. What these seminary students experience in a weekend retreat is what the small, ecumenical community residing here year-round strives for constantly: a balance between reaching inward and outward, between quiet attention to one's own journey and active ministry in the world. It is work that begins in faith. Jesus took time away from the crowds to go "up to a lonely place;" he role-models a healthy means for us to sustain our own efforts. Those who join the community come from a spectrum of religious traditions, mostly Christian, and stay for varying lengths of time. Our commitment is the same: to live on the earth with care, to pray constantly, work radically, and create sacred space for others' reflection. How, we ask, can faith shape our every choice, in lifestyle and occupation and relationships? In other words, how can we live from the center of our belief? At this moment, the chaos of food scraps and unwashed dishes on the counter speaks to the challenge.

The seminarians will eat silently indoors while a second group—a dozen or so volunteers here to split and stack wood—picnics on the lawn. Our big cedar log lodge uses wood for heat over the winter, but recently two years' worth of firewood was lost when the maintenance building, ignited by a manufacturer defect in a car, burned to the ground. The wood must be replaced before cold sets in. All morning the volunteers have been laboring with an air of necessity down by the wood shed. They are an extension of the resident community, committed to the patterns of simple living and the importance of retreat in spiritual growth. In some hidden way, this piece of property, tucked in the Minnesota woods, or the friendly bustle of the community, or the deep quiet of time spent in solitude here has touched their lives, and they offer their thanks in the form of service. Their connection is evidence that what peace is found here spills outward in ever-widening concentric ripples, working for change in the wider world.

The noise of chopping vegetables, timers, and our last minute panic spills into the dining room. I hope the students understand these as the sounds that make reflective quiet possible. Scott, whose shirt is splattered with potato-cheese soup, rings the outdoor bell for lunch. Its brassy tone carries over the yard, beyond the creek and the stand of Norwegian pines. The volunteers stomp into the house with dirty hands and sweat-streaked faces.

I heap the broccoli salad into big ceramic bowls: sweet onions, sunflower seeds, raisins, a creamy dressing of mayonnaise, sugar and vinegar. There is so much salad it looks like it could feed, as my mother would say, a veritable army. I stir with a wooden spoon until the flowerlets and broccoli stems are shiny. Sue, my spiritual director, has told me that there are six tastes: bitter, sweet, sour, salt, spice and satisfaction. It is the cook's attentiveness that results in satisfaction. As much as I am able, I have sliced, measured, and stirred with intention. In this place of prayerful retreat, where behind the scenes it grows hectic, I want to recognize those small things that nurture our souls. I pray that the salad— along with soup, homemade rye bread, and ginger snap cookies—will sustain us for an afternoon of hauling and stacking logs, becoming energy stored in wood to warm us through the winter. I pray that the meal will feed the meditations of tree-climbing, silent seminarians.

What interests me is how spirit imbeds itself in the substance of the world. The broccoli has turned my hands purple. When I bring my fingers to my nose there is a pungent, grainy smell that lingers for the rest of the day.

Outside, under the autumn sky, I join the volunteers for lunch. We sit at rickety picnic tables, careful not to suddenly leave the bench for fear the others will go flying. The sun is warm on our necks. We sing grace raucously, teasing the more contemplative diners indoors with our enthusiasm. And then we pass the bread.

The woman sitting next to me is here for the first time. Her curly black hair is held back from her face with a blue bandanna and there are freckles on her nose. Her friend, who lived in the community some time back, introduces her as Melissa. Melissa squints in the sunlight.

"Thanks for helping today," I tell her.

"Oh, it's great to be outside," she says. Her cheeks are red with the cold air and hard work. "All week I'm in an office without windows. I love the exercise of splitting wood." She pauses to absent-mindedly stir her soup, then tilts her head toward me in a curious angle. "I'm really interested, if you don't mind telling me—how is it that you came to be here?"

Without looking I can feel MaryJo, who also lives in the community, smirk from across the table. I kick her foot under the bench. Every guest, every prospective resident, every visitor asks us this question. Answering becomes a chore. It's a good question. Lurking under its conversational surface is a desire for story—soul story, the meat and blood of a life. Really Melissa is asking, "What kind of a journey led you to this contemplative community? How has this place shaped you? And who, after all, is your God?" At the beginning of lunch time pleasantries, before the broccoli salad has made it around the table, this question leaves me tongue-tied.

I see myself in this woman. She is asking what I want to ask every person I know whose spiritual life is textured, not simply by tradition or a moral practice or intellectual exercises, but by a fresh and individual relationship with divinity. *What is your experience of spirit?* The old stories about God, contained within the covers of the Bible and the boundaries of church doctrine, no longer satisfy me. I love these stories and how, over a lifetime of hearing them on Sunday mornings, they have worked their way into the soft substance of my bones. But most times a bridge is missing, a translation from the historical, mythical page to the realities of my busy day. What does it mean to talk with God, to discern one's calling, to serve others with faith and commitment—here and now, in *this* body, balanced on the edge of an unstable picnic bench, in *this* place with the kitchen door to my left, the sun overhead, and the bountiful garden going to seed at my right? I ache for life-stories that cross the gap from the mundane to mystery with language that is down-to-earth, alive, and gripping.

I search for these stories because I want to grow in my relationship with God and often don't know what that means. During worship services I listen carefully to the prayers, tentative and brief, that community members offer. I cross-examine their theology while we do dishes: "What do you believe about incarnation?" I ask. "About why bad things happen? About resurrection?" When Sue tells me what it was like to climb Kilimanjaro as a celebration of graduating from seminary at age fifty-five, I hungrily take in her story. "It was like scaling the face of God," she says, with thrill and terror in her eyes. I read voraciously, looking for a story grounded in the particulars of a complicated life yet striving after fundamental truths. At meals, when the retreats we host are not silent, I question our guests much as Melissa questions me. I want to hear an honest experience of a spiritual journey. How do these earthly vessels we walk around in relate us to divinity? Perhaps if I listen carefully enough I will identify in another's story that tiny electric synapse—a leap in space and time—that links what is flesh to what is eternal. I suspect this is what also links others to me and me to my God.

I push the salad around my plate with a fork and wonder if the seminary group, dining in monastic silence, isn't having an easier meal. The stories that satisfy me are few and far between. What it means to be on a spiritual journey remains essentially enigmatic.

When I answer Melissa's question, I can understand why. The response I give her is far from adequate. "Oh, I don't mind telling you," I say. "I was teaching seventh grade English and found that it sapped all my creative energy." Melissa rolls her eyes at the mention of seventh grade, showing me she understands. "I wanted to live with integrity, to work from my center. I wanted to write. I figured that the ordinary work of running a retreat center would nurture my creative life and spiritual life instead of draining them."

"And has it?" she asks. She has grown distracted; I can tell by the way she looks past me toward the bird feeder, where nuthatches flutter.

"Yes." It's a long story. What more can I say within the confines of a picnic?

I have failed Melissa as others have failed me, by giving a summary and not a story. I have not told her about bedtime as a child when my mother taught me to pray; I have not described that dusky moment at the edge of a railway platform in Wales before stepping into a journey through solitude. The horrible foreboding that comes over me in Sue's spiritual direction room, that my well-organized life is being ravaged by something far more wonderful, I keep to myself. I don't tell her how I first grieved my infant nephew's death in this place, or that the fire that took the wood she's replacing also took my belongings. Maddeningly enough, I withhold from her the primary reason I came here: my determination to live out as a bisexual woman. With Melissa—with most people, even those I care for deeply, I now realize—I omit the details that signal truth. Details require words that are raw, outside the bounds of acceptable table conversation. They scrape at the essence of an instant and bring it into painful view. Within a story, the details are what leap from the teller's to the listener's heart. Without details, we avoid intimacy and we inhibit revelation.

I want to tell Melissa my story. She is jabbing at broccoli spears on her plate and shielding her eyes from the sun. I want to put words to my journey from its beginning to this present moment, which is by no means an end. I suspect that I have been unsuccessful at finding stories that speak to me because they have been in hiding. "What would happen if one woman told the truth about her life?" Muriel Rukeyser asked. "The world would split open." Her answer has become a rallying cry for transformation: Telling our stories is an act of resistance against institutions that would rather tell stories about us. It is also how we can bear witness to God's love imbedded in our lives. Perhaps in telling my story I can crack open the mystery of being both spark of spirit and creation of earth.

Back in the kitchen the seminary students are bringing their dishes to the sink. Restaurant plates clatter and glass clinks on glass, but there is no talking—strange with so many people in a dirty kitchen. When a few break the silence to whisper thanks for lunch, I smile back. A meal has united us, however briefly. I squirt soap into the dish pan and set the hot water running. Over the sink, thumb-tacked to the bulletin board, is my dish-washing meditation:

> Doing the dishes is like washing a baby Buddha.
> The profane is sacred.
> Everyday mind is Buddha's mind.
> —Thich N'hat Hanh

This is a far more difficult meditation than my last, which was from Agatha Christie: "I plan my next book while doing the dishes." The dishcloth slips into a drinking glass and I sweep it around in a second. There are forty drinking glasses, and plates and bowls and silver; there is a towering pile of pots and mixing bowls. The meditation demands that I remain on the lookout. If each dish can be a baby Buddha, then God might reside anywhere—in Scott, my fellow community member, who is tone-deaf yet pretends to sing lugubrious Gregorian chants after the silent guests clear out; in the weedy garden outside the kitchen window; in these details of my utterly un-noteworthy days. The skin of my fingers grows soft with water wrinkles. I still find myself planning a book, but it is quite ordinary. There is no mystical ecstasy, no wild sex scene, no original insight into living well. There is only the dailiness of a profane life straining after what is sacred.

I see Sue for spiritual direction down in the city every month. Above the sofa where I sit hangs a Chinese ink and wash painting, two feet wide and three feet long. It pulls your eye first to the upper left corner, where there is vertical calligraphy and the artist's chop. Your eye travels down a blurred mountain slope into a foggy valley and then up the opposite side. Beneath a grove of evergreens on the far right is what looks like a tea house with simple, curved eaves and a window facing the valley. A man sits inside writing a book. Out in the center of the painting, halfway between the mountains and suspended in mist, there is another man. He is walking on air. He is not hovering and is by no means ghostlike. He is solid and his walk is determined.

On the day three years ago when I told Sue I would give up my job teaching in order to be open about my sexual identity, intentional about my spiritual life and committed to my writing, she nodded to the wall behind me. "You will be like that man in the small house," she said. I turned my back to her and took in the painting's ease and determination. The man bends over his work, but his face is raised to the window. "Your soul is out there," Sue said, pointing to the walking man, "and your writing life will reach out to it." I looked from the window of the tea house out over the enormity of mist and mountains, the mysterious realm where spirits walk. An invisible suspension line connects the man on solid ground with the man striding across nothing. There is unity in the painting because they are the same man.

I am beginning to see that what spans the distance between flesh and spirit is the creative act—the painting leaping into my soul's landscape, the book being written, the person we become when we risk everything for the sake of growing. I don't need to tell my story simply to discover God residing in the details. It's also a matter of participating in creation, calling out of chaos the ten-fingered, heart-beating world that is my life. This here, between these covers, is an experienced relationship with spirit. I will wash dishes, and I will tell you a story.

That day in Sue's office, I nodded up toward the corner of the painting. "What does the calligraphy say?" I asked her, knowing full well that she doesn't read Chinese. I love to watch her use her imagination.

Sue grinned at me, eyes glinting. "It says, 'Elizabeth is on a journey . . . .'"

A Childhood

"Rose-trees," said Mary. "Are there rose-trees?"

Ben Weatherstaff took up his spade and began to dig.

"There was ten year' ago," he mumbled.

"I should like to see them," said Mary. "Where is the green door? There must be a door somewhere."

Ben drove his spade deep and looked as uncompanionable as he had looked when she first saw him.

"There was ten year' ago, but there isn't now," he said.

"No door!" cried Mary. "There must be."

Outside the retreat center's chapel one day is a pair of shoes. I walk past them on my way to empty the first floor waste baskets. But then I stop and turn around. These shoes are tucked in the corner beside the door-frame and hymnal bookshelf. Flat soled, black canvas, they are open vessels lapping up the silence that seeps under the door. People are praying in there. I bend down to look at these shoes more closely. Their rims are stitched with thread, and the elastic pieces that cross their tops pull the sides tight. With my hand, hesitantly, I reach in to touch the smooth instep. The shoes surprise me by seeming faithful, a quality I don't usually attribute to things.

I've never given much attention to my own shoes. When I was growing up, my family removed their shoes in the house, a pile always disorderly and growing beside the front door. My sister and I levered them off with our toes even before shedding our jackets. "Guests will think this is a shoe store," my mother complained. I don't think she minded, though. The grit that lodged itself in the tread of our sneakers stayed confined to the entryway. We raced around the house in our stocking feet, touching the iron railing by the stairs for the sharp blue electrical shocks we could see in the dark.

Shoes carried my family out into the world. My younger sister's were full of holes and drawn on with magic marker, much to my parents' chagrin. Mine were proper—dark leather, worn at the heels where I dragged my feet. They walked with me the five blocks to the bus stop, through the scuffed school corridors, down the steep streets of Tarrytown, New York, with a quick visit to the Hanzarides' doughnut shop for a nibble and a look at the men's Greek noses, to Wednesday church school. In the sanctuary they raced with me as I played tag between the pews. Once, on a dare, I climbed the fire escape to the roof of the church; I looked down, down, over the tips of my loafers to the old town streets with hardware shops and Hispanic groceries, over the sloped brick buildings, down to the train station, the GM plant with acres of sparkling cars, down to the steel-grey river lying face-open to the sun. And then I grew dizzy.

Polished shoes strode stiffly with my father to the YMCA early in the morning, where he placed them in a locker and walked barefoot into the pool. He swam laps, a steady, unrushed crawl, while steam rose to the iron rafters. His shoes then took him to the corporate office where he practiced law. Fashionable, mildly practical shoes took long steps with my mother from the Girl Scout Council to PTA to the Sunday school room, then back home in time to greet Marcy and me after school. They pressed the gas pedal of her automatic Volvo as she shuffled us to our various afternoon commitments. In church, they stood firm when she rose to sing the hymns. Her voice was strong.

My family wore our shoes without consideration, oblivious to the material means by which the immaterial things we prized so highly—our connection to the community, our work, our education—were made possible. We polished, laced and buckled shoes because they were natural, public extensions of ourselves.

These black canvas shoes waiting patiently outside the chapel door remind me that where we take off our shoes is holy ground. Surely the pile beside the front door of my childhood is a clue. I want to travel in and out of the intimacies of the past, growing worn and comfortable, until I find myself at the doorstep of mystery. For a while I need to dwell in that old home again, sliding on the kitchen tiles and racing across the cold basement floor. I also need to journey out, into the back yard beside the rolling Hudson River, into the lonely classrooms and the church sanctuary which also formed me. The God of shoes is divinity in motion. Over time, the instep softens to the shape of a single foot. If I can know what carried me here, bending down to these well-worn shoes at the chapel door, then I will also know what walks forward with me, out of the closet into the gravel and sinking soil of the world.

I spot the black canvas shoes on a woman's feet at noon when I am serving tea to the guests. She is a Catholic sister; her hair is white and stylish, brushed back from her clear face, and she is wearing a plain blue sweater. When she asks my name, I see her eyes are grey. At my response she exclaims, "Oh! *You're* the Elizabeth I've been praying for!" She means since the garage fire, which destroyed my belongings, but she could have been there my whole life, kneeling stocking-footed in the chapel, mothering my spirit from a thousand miles away. Her fingers, holding a cup out so I can fill it, are thin. What can I possibly say? I pour tea for her, spicy and orange. I suspect prayer of working backward and forward in time, of touching our lives as secretly as I touched her shoes, and of slowly changing us.

She reminds me of a monk I saw but never met when I was nine.

My family and aunt had spent a February weekend skiing in Weston, Vermont, and on Sunday attended mass at the Benedictine monastery. The small chapel was packed. Sitting cross-legged on a bench along the far wall, I strained to see the monks—a species I'd never encountered in my Methodist upbringing. How peculiar it was that men would devote their lives to God and walk around wearing robes! One played the guitar while the others sang. When the scripture was read, I heard their love for the Word rather than the words themselves. Morning sun lighted on stone walls. There was one blue-eyed, elderly monk I could see through the crowd. His white hair was a bit on end, as though he'd forgotten to smooth it down after ducking into his robe. He seemed to me very, very old. His face was wrinkled with prayer. For a moment he looked at me, and then moved his gaze.

That look shook me to the core. I was a child, and this holy man had looked into my eyes. He seemed to recognize an essential part of my identity that I didn't yet know existed.

At that time, consciousness was just beginning to bubble up to the surface of my awareness. One day at school I had eaten my bag lunch in the late spring heat of the fourth grade classroom instead of the cafeteria. I remember peering through the window's glare onto the playground where my classmates were playing dodge ball. Between them and myself seemed an unbridgeable distance, two stories of the old brick elementary school, and suddenly it occurred to me that *I had thoughts*, that this textured dialogue with God ran continuously in my head. It was a moment of great discovery, filled with sadness and fear. If I had thoughts, then I was independent (which I assumed meant *different*) from the others—from those I considered my friends simply because I spent time with them, from my mediocre but well-meaning teachers, even from my family. I have never been more lonely. At home I cried for hours into my mother's lap, her pleas to know what was wrong making me cry harder because I didn't know, I couldn't articulate it. I felt so close to her and so infinitely far away.

Perhaps it was in my imagination that the kind-faced monk was praying for me, for me alone in the whole world. It doesn't much matter if it was true or if I made it up, because the results are the same. I sat on the bench, my feet tucked under my Sunday skirt, believing completely that with that one brief glance the brother had blessed me. After the service I was buried in the crowd of tall adults and didn't even get to touch his hand. But I found, in the priory gift shop, something to help me remember: a sterling dove on a black cord, hand-crafted by one of the brothers. I paid fifteen dollars of my allowance for it, hoping my parents wouldn't ask why. Its wings were rounded, and if I held it pointing downward they looked like pentecostal flames. When I slipped it over my head and under my shirt, the cold silver touched my bony chest. It bounced there the entire car ride home, in the back seat of my parents' station wagon.

I am certain that all our deepest longings have their roots in childhood, and that discernment of God's movement involves digging them up to expose their soiled, organic forms. Sue asks me, her face serious, what I most wanted to be when I was a child. While I was still oblivious to the obvious hindrances—that I was female, I wasn't Catholic, I wasn't even straight—I wanted to be a monk. Their life of prayer sparked my fancy. I thought about it daily, from fourth grade through graduation, as, after my morning shower, I lifted the black cord from the shelf beside the sink over my head, ducking in a reverential nod. God was like that kind-faced monk, and God could connect me to others. At school I wondered if my relationship with God peeked out through my interactions with peers or in my class work, the way the black cord sometimes exposed itself along my neckline. In bed at night, clutching the dove for comfort, I didn't pray to Jesus or to the Father God but to the Spirit who could fly with ease from my soul to the monk's, or to my father when he was in the hospital, or to the black-haired girl in my art class with whom I was very much in love. What went unspoken during daylight could be released at night. If prayer was the work of monks, I wanted a part.

But I also wanted to write. When I picked up a pen and notebook, I wrote with a dark fervor for which there was no other outlet. I loved that all-encompassing engagement with the page, that place of ultimate permission. I undertook my first full-length novel when I was eleven. It was a woeful tale of a young girl whose artistic proclivities went unrecognized by her family. Late one rainy night, furtively, she boarded a train for Vermont, watched the wet countryside slide past, and disembarked in a small town. Wind drove the rain at a slant; she walked five miles in that torrent up the mountain to the priory. Soaked and shivering, she pulled the bell at the front gate. After what seemed like forever, a monk with tussled hair arrived, holding a torch above his head and frowning. He pulled her in from the rain, sat her before an open fire and put a blanket around her shoulders, all without speaking a word. The monks understood, and took her into their fold. Of course she became the monastery's favorite, making everyone chuckle by wearing a monk's robe and worshipping with her serious, knit brow. They taught her to paint and sing, and were astonished at her brilliance. The novel broke down at that point because her life was as perfect as I could imagine. It sat in a folder on my bed-stand, a secret, and no one ever read it before it burned.

Adults, impatient with my child self and preferring to know me once I'd graduated to full-fledged personhood, asked what I wanted to be when I grew up. I knew enough to not speak the truth—monkhood was not a practical career option. Instead, I talked in a half-teasing manner about becoming a hermit. "That's a lonely existence," my mother said, and I knew she was right despite my proclivity for solitude. Later I buried my dream of becoming a writer in the same way, under talk about teaching so practical that I eventually persuaded myself. When I think today of my childhood depressions (the hours I spent weeping into my mother's lap, the days I roamed the high school halls, numb but on the brink of tears), I can't help wondering if they sprang, if only in part, from this resignation, that what I most wanted I would never have. A life of prose and prayer was simply not a viable option for a young Protestant girl.

The origin of my relationship with God lurks in what went unspoken in my family. We kept quiet about the Sacred; words might endanger us by giving Spirit a substance or form we'd have to look at head on, unblinking. The act of naming was powerful, and so I was taught to shun it. Even today I hesitate, unwilling to choose words to describe God for fear I will, as is inevitable, fall short, or worse, defile something too magnificent for names. This is dangerous work.

In my family, faith was a strong, silent undercurrent not unlike the Hudson at the edge of our back yard. Faith was one of those qualities of being, like modesty and a love of learning, that my sister and I absorbed from our parents. What we knew first, even before words, was blind trust, ignorance of suffering, my mother's hope that her daughters' gender would not hinder them and my father's conviction that we would have a place in the world without having to prove ourselves, as he had, climbing out of the New York Italian ghetto. My mother was seminary educated and my father was a lawyer, but I don't think either could articulate what it was they believed. Belief in its essence defied words. Both of my parents knew a loving presence in their lives and assumed we knew the same. This knowing became my rock.

It was my mother who taught me to pray. When she put me to bed she sat at my left side, her thigh touching my thigh, her body turned to face me. The stripes of the bedcovers—zigzags of blue, green and red—rose in a small bump at my feet, traveled up skinny legs and ended in a tuck under my chin. I was three years old, or five, or eight. The neck of the teddy bear under my arm had been resewn tightly to his body; his paws were worn smooth. My mother leaned slightly against me, placing the book we were reading on my knees. She had embroidered the wall-hanging that filled the space over my bed: rabbits leaping across a green field. As my mother read I watched the round-tailed one in the corner, ready to pounce. Her voice wrapped stories around me, stories with no content except warmth and the slow unrolling of sound. I watched the white rabbit caught mid-jump over the grassy center of my wall and wondered what it would be like to fly.

My mother coached me through prayer so regularly that I believed it was one of those rituals we do to stay alive, like brushing teeth and eating three meals a day. "What are you thankful for?" she asked. She was confident with the question and with our movement into sacred time; it never occurred to me that we had crossed a boundary. I began the dialogue: "Dear God. Thank you for the club Linny and I built down by the swamp. Thank you that Mommy made cheese noodles for dinner. . . . " I thought God was like Teddy, under my arm. He absorbed love, tears, and all the words I spoke to him. My mother interjected her own prayers on my behalf: "Thank you that Beth has been given Mrs. Swinsy, who is a good teacher; thank you that we've all finally gotten over that flu-bug." We closed together with prayers of intercession so simple that they became for me a formula for sleep: "God bless Mommy and Daddy and Marcy and Beth, and all our friends and relatives, especially—," the litany of those we cared for, animal and human alike, as though God's blessing were a blanket thrown over us for warmth through the night.

My mother sang to me then, "The Riddle Song," "Lavender's Blue, Dilly-Dilly," or "Swing Low, Sweet Chariot." I pictured myself working in a cotton field, then lifted from my labors by a shining, large-wheeled wagon. My mother's voice was untrained but utterly true. She never sang without attending to the song's meaning. My favorite was "In the Bleak Midwinter," which I requested year-round. I imagined the grey and ice at Jesus' birth, and I could hear my mother wondering the same question as the writer of the song: "What can I give him, poor as I am?" The answer was at once easy and difficult. "If I were a shepherd, I would bring a lamb. If I were a wise man, I would do my part. But what can I give him? Give him my heart." I wished to be a shepherd or a wise man, because my heart seemed a fearful present. It was too small a gift for the Christ child, and yet too huge for me to relinquish.

When I grew old enough that, my mother felt, I could say prayers on my own, the intimate window into my mother's prayer life closed. Since then, I have never heard her pray more than a rote blessing at mealtimes. I think she is shy, preferring to hide what she knows of the sacred in the patterned cross-stitch always unfolding between her fingers, in her baked goods, in her work with small children. Or perhaps she is ashamed of the simplicity of her prayer. I was. In junior high confirmation, I realized that I still chatted with God like a baby and was horrified. *That* couldn't be prayer. Prayer was supposed to be high and holy, formal the way we dressed up on Sunday mornings, petition and repentance, so be it and amen. Now I yearn for the kind of faith that doesn't question God's part in the dialogue, where God is more imaginary friend than distant deity. I want to move back in time; I want to learn again those first intimate whispers my mother called prayer.

Most likely, though, my preadolescence made my mother self-conscious and therefore distrustful of words to convey her spirit's movement. Words may come out stilted, formulaic, or, worst of all, evangelical, and so they are apt to betray a deep knowing of God. Better to guard this by not speaking at all. When my mother and I stopped sharing prayer, God was forced underground into the silence of our individual lives and into the public formulas of creed and liturgy. If I wanted to preserve a personal relationship with God, I was on my own.

I had another evening ritual that began when I was five and continued through adolescence. In bed at night, impatient for dreams, I told myself stories. I imagined myself back on the playground swing, pumping so high that I soared into another world where people grew wings and rode on clouds. There was no distinction between the end of my stories and the beginning of dreams, so the plots grew wild and mythic. The children I knew acquired adult faces. The river ran over its banks, flooded the streets, and I had to swim to school holding my pencil case above the water so I'd still be able to write. Every night God asked me what kind of dream I'd like to have, and where my narrative stumbled with half-consciousness, some braver story-teller took over.

Without my mother's guidance, the boundaries between prayer and my imaginary life blurred. I read just one more chapter of the Arthurian legends, my flashlight's beam swimming rhythmically through the dark, and then I pulled the sheets up to my chin. I began with "Dear God" the way I was supposed to, but soon the people populating my prayers appeared wearing medieval garb; we brushed through the forest in search of the wise hermit who sat under tall, groaning pines. Prayer, story, and the wilderness of dreams were indistinct. An airy narrative blew through them all. Crinoline curtains danced ghostlike over my bed.

In junior high, when religion became concrete—a clear delineation between right and wrong—prayer, I decided, was prayer, and story was story. One was holy and the other not. If the truth be known, my talks with God had become repetitive, mostly my own whining requests. "Please let Mr. Polliche understand the meaning of my poem. Help Julie not be so crabby about her parents' divorce. Why must Miguel have the locker next to me?" God was lax in his half of the dialogue. Because I was determined to be a profound child, prayer became an exercise of will. Only once I released myself from duty with an impatient "amen" was I free. My stories, then, were filled with intrigue, art and sex. I strolled a flower garden with a blind woman, touching the petals of tiger lilies and snapdragons. We performed fire-lit rituals at Stonehenge. I fell in love with a gentle, bearded man who looked like my seventh grade teacher and we consummated our marriage in full sunlight.

Eventually I gave up trying to be good. Surely God must have been as bored with our conversation as I was. Instead of "amen," I ended prayer with, "Let me tell you a story"; I led God by the hand into that other, colorful world we both created. Today, remembering this, I know of no better way to communicate with God. The soul we all share hungers for stories. Our stories, lifted up to the night, onto the page, into the ear of another, are prayer.

When I was young, I wanted more than anything to be in relationship with mystery. I wanted to dive under the ropes, heavy with seaweed, that sectioned off the Phillips Manor swimming area, and encounter the current where the Hudson River is forty-one feet deep at high tide. Instead I hung on to the styrofoam buoy, slippery and green, rising on the crests and falling into the troughs. The river was unfathomable. Ducking under the surface, I dug my toes in the murky bottom and suspended my weightless body in the olive underworld for as long as I could hold my breath.

Linny was my best friend. We spent much of our summers in my basement where it was cool, enacting a drama called "Spirit and a Half," in which we could share our souls in order to have energy to withstand the evil queen we served—an amusement park red and white teddy bear, almost as tall as we were and not the least bit huggable. When one of us, bedecked in the tatters of my mother's prom dress, had to encounter Her Majesty, the other transferred her strength and courage by holding up her empty palms. The giver was left with half a spirit, and endured much pain because of it.

One time Linny was on her knees. I had given her half my spirit and lay on the rug contorted by the injury this caused. I felt certain that our friendship was worth suffering for, because Linny would be able to survive her audience with the queen and we could again frolic together at the village dance. Where taffeta touched Linny's neck her skin turned red; she bowed her head in gratitude. She wept bitterly, earnestly, at my sacrifice and the devotion it signified.

Suddenly we snapped out of it. We broke into fits of nervous laughter. We had been *there*; we had crossed over and made that world *real*. The question I most wanted answered as child was: *How are we connected?* Linny and I imagined these fluid spirits that we could share or withhold at will. Her tears were proof that they existed.

In junior high, when Linny drifted off to become popular, I disappeared into books, an open paperback my best shield against the cruel looks and knowing comments in the corridors. I was plain and unwilling to buckle under to peer pressure to do something about it. My few friendships were fierce: Magriet, Olinda, Julie . . . odd, smart girls, under- and over-developed, with swift wits and bookish inclinations. Together we signed a pact to someday become geniuses. We stood united against the more socially adept cliques and passed our favorite paperbacks down rows of desks the way others passed notes. At lunch-time we skipped out of the cafeteria to eat in the English classroom, playing jacks on the smooth, wooden floor. In math class we grew swift with formulas so we could put their irrelevant texts aside—what could possibly interest us in a subject with answers?—for the latest novel.

I was obsessed with the tales and language of King Arthur. "All around them was the stillness of the nighttime," Howard Pyle narrated to me in the threadbare hardcover of our school library. "And overhead and about them lay the silent whiteness of the effulgent moon. And the shadows of each and the shadows of the horse of each followed them across the moorland, very black and mysterious." Overtly I didn't think Merlin existed or that Camelot ever raised its banners. But I believed the tales the same way I was taught by my liberal-minded parents to believe the Bible, reading the impulse behind the words and distrusting the facts. It didn't matter whether Merlin waved his wand to create Stonehenge out of a violent storm or Neolithic engineers dragged the bluestones all the way from the Welsh mountains; either way, there was this place of power, aligned with the stars, that communicated with mystery. The quest for the holy grail taught me that when something sacred is on the loose, you drop everything and scatter across the countryside in order to find it.

In high school, my own quest led me to sometimes forego the school bus and walk two and a half miles home. I heaved my book bag over my shoulder and walked alone down the hill to the river. At the small, stone-arched railroad station I turned aside into Kingsland Point Park, an outcrop of land by the old lighthouse behind the GM plant. There was a jetty of dynamited granite that extended fifty feet into the tide, and a chain-link fence prohibiting fishermen and high school partiers. I exempted myself. I dumped my books, balanced my way out on the rocks, swung around the final pole, and balanced my way back. Taking off my shoes, I leapt from the restraining wall onto an unused beach. The sand felt chilly that late in the afternoon.

I sat on a washed-up log and wrote poems, straining to touch the pulse of the river. I wanted all my loneliness, my effort in school, involvement in activities and love of writing to have some meaning; I wanted to swim where the river was most swift, where I might touch the heart of God. Gradually, I came to feel that the water and I shared a secret—my poems were love poems and the river lapped them up the same way I absorbed the waves' sounds: deeply, endearingly. I knew that during lectures at school, running errands with my mother, or on the football field at commencement, I'd only have to look out over the steepled town to that shimmering expanse to be comforted by the river's enduring presence. I might never find meaning, but there'd always be relationship.

The only crisis that marred my childhood and challenged my family's faith happened when I was twelve. My father's kidneys failed. The cause was unknown—"idiopathic," he told Marcy and me, "meaning the doctor's an idiot and the patient's pathetic." He kept his pain out of our sight, his face never betraying any loss of control. But a cloud of worry settled over the house anyhow. It sprung from my mother's brow and the tight way she held her shoulders. I knew, had we still been praying together, that my mother would have offered special prayers for my father, and so alone in bed at night I sent pleas to God: Make him better, make him better. There was nothing else I could do.

The doctors operated on his wrist to create a fistula, an artery connected to a vein so the blood by-passed his left hand and made all its vessels pop up and throb. When I placed my fingers on his bulging veins, it felt like one of those trick handshake buzzers that make you jump. It was called a thrill, he told us, because he was so thrilling. We stood beside his hospital chair as he stuck heavy needles into the thrill and taped them to his arm. We watched his blood travel down the tube, loop into a big machine pretending it was a kidney and then travel back into his veins. The hospital floor was cold; the machine made a great whirring noise. Three times a week my father's blood was outside of his body. It was monstrous. I was afraid to visit him.

When the doctors moved my father from hemodialysis to peritoneal dialysis, allowing him to wash his stomach's lining on his own four times a day, the reality of his illness came home. Boxes of saline solution lined the basement walls, a doctor's scale with real weights appeared in my parents' bathroom, and my father kept blood pressure equipment in his underwear drawer. Hooks sprang up above my father's favorite chairs where he hung bags of saline; the liquid drained into a tube that entered his belly while he read the *New York Times*. If I stood near him when he changed tubes, I had to wear a surgical mask. Dialysis became a rhythm that structured our time, familiar but never comfortable.

Soon it seemed like I'd never known anything other than a life of crisis. My father was on a waiting list for kidney donors; we tensed up in expectation every time the phone rang. Transplant surgery terrified us because it would break our safe rhythm with more enormous risk. But it was our only hope for returning to normal. I couldn't remember normal. All I'd ever known was unbearable waiting and being good so as not to upset my mother. Marcy and I cried often without understanding why.

After seven months the phone call finally came: a young woman had died in a car accident and my father would receive one of her kidneys. He drove himself down to the hospital in the Bronx, still dressed in his business suit. The surgery went smoothly. They placed the extra kidney beside my father's stomach and after a few weeks sent him home with a calendar packed with appointments and enough pills to fill a medicine cabinet. He was alive, independent of machines. The random hooks disappeared from around the house, and my father used his extra organ as an excuse for a slight beer belly.

A year later we celebrated his kidney's first anniversary at the Russian Tea Room. The maitre'd helped me out of my coat at the door, making me blush, and the baklava, already dripping, was served with a pitcher of honey. It was an extravagant evening, warm with candlelight. My father glowed with life. The strain and pressure of the past two years had knit us that much closer and lifted our happiness to a familial elation. I remember the dark drive home from the city and the phone ringing as we opened the front door. It was the hospital with test results: my father's body was rejecting the organ. At midnight he drove back down to the Bronx, where they figured out otherwise—the hospital had fed him bad blood and he'd contracted syphilis, treatable early on with penicillin. One phone call unseated our new confidence. It seemed the ordeal might never end.

I was an early adolescent, and believed in a magic formula: If I refused to acknowledge in words or in my consciousness the possibility of tragedy, then God would not let it happen. That my father might die, not only after the failure but for years after the transplant, loomed large but was unspeakable in our household. In the end, everything worked the way we had hoped; my father was healthy after a rocky couple of years, thanks to an anonymous woman's generosity. On a deeper level, however, I never reconciled my trust in God's goodness with the bare fact that disaster *had* struck. There was no explanation for the kidney failure. If nature had followed its course, my dad would have died.

Something inside of me was different as a result. I was still shy; I still turned inward for solace, hid behind long bangs, and never spoke more in front of adults than was necessary. Yet I willed myself to abandon reticence. I passed out donor cards to my friends, encouraging them to sign their organs away. I knew that in an instant anyone might die or be transformed forever, and so I vowed always, *always* to tell others when I loved them. Perhaps this was what Jesus meant by the kingdom of God being at hand—the only opportunity for connection was *now*. I wrote Christmas cards in a fervor of adolescent honesty, even confessing to Mr. Polliche, my bearded, poetry-loving English teacher, how much he meant to me. I promised myself I'd always put words to my feelings, and, no matter how sentimental it felt, I would never be ashamed. Life was not going to wait for me to grow brave or eloquent. Love, I decided, exists in the present and should be shared recklessly.

The congregation I grew up in still worships on Washington Street, a half mile up the hill from the river and a block from the fire house whose horn blasts into Sunday services. Methodist, built in 1837, the building is brick with peeling white trim. Five steps lead up to the double doors, which are nine feet tall and so heavy they take two hands to open. Inside is the dusty smell of well-worn, red horsehair carpeting and streaks of colored sunlight. I know the building as a child does; I know the soft patches of carpet beneath the pews; I know how the heat vents in the aisle will balloon your skirt with warm air; I know if you climb a ladder above the back hallway, you enter a forest of organ pipes, some tall silvery trunks, some penny whistles sprouting in rows like saplings. I know the packed-dirt floor of the tenpin alley underneath the kitchen and the choking pink smell of the women's bathroom, quite distinct from the men's room's molding green. I know the best hiding places and a story for every stained glass window. After communion Sundays, I approached the altar, blew out the candles, and tore a large chunk—an eatable size—of my mother's home-baked bread. I knew what was sacred about that place and what was infinitely ordinary.

The church was my second home, where I was cared for by doting, elderly women, by the ungainly pastors who passed through our doors every few years, and by the ultimate Parent who acquired there a gender and omnipotent personality. On Wednesday afternoons we left school early to cram into the back of my mother's station wagon and go to religious education, and on Sunday mornings we paraded out of the sanctuary after the children's sermon, stomping downstairs to the classrooms. In the finished part of the church basement, among coloring books and felt story-boards, God grew a white beard and Jesus walked around in sandals, with arms awkwardly outstretched toward us children. We learned religion like a vocabulary lesson, filling in the mid-sentence blanks in our textbooks with unsharpened pew pencils. The facts from those lessons escaped me. But the resonant souls of New Testament stories seeped into my psyche: God's dove descending on the baptized Jesus; Jesus spitting to make healing mud; Jesus going up to a lonely place. Jesus, the prophet unaccepted in his home town, was a comfort to me, not because I was prophetic but because I often felt unaccepted. If Jesus knew rejection and cared for the rejected, I could love him.

The Sunday school had a Time-Out space that was my mother's response to unruly children: a refrigerator box painted on the inside with our rainbows and crude Christian icons against a sky-blue background. It was a coveted refuge to which we could retreat whenever we chose or our teachers chose for us. Curled inside on the floor pillow, my heartbeat slowing, I came to understand in an unconscious way why Jesus "withdrew from the crowds to pray." Space and time apart, even separated by flimsy walls of cardboard, were necessary to hear God's still, calming voice.

At Easter the Sunday school mothers provided us with milky filmstrips and colored pencils. We were to illustrate Jesus' life and narrate it as we hand-cranked the film through the projector. As tiny as we could, we drew the manger scene, the child protégé in the temple, Jesus walking on water. We drew the last supper as we knew it, all twelve disciples lined up on one side of the dinner table. We drew the stone rolling away. In the last frame, where "The End" belonged, I wrote "The Beginning" instead in my unsteady fourth-grade script. It made the teacher raise her eyebrows. I understood early on that a good story has a surprising twist at the end that should make the reader's heart leap. It was remarkably clever of God to have Jesus' death bring us new life. I learned to trust God, not as the parent who was willing to sacrifice his child to rectify human sin, but as the master storyteller.

Rarely did adults bother to ask what I already knew of God from my experience. Instead, they proceeded to teach me what I ought to believe, and so what happened in church—especially what happened Sunday mornings, as the pastor droned on and I counted the squares of grating that covered the organ pipes—was distinct from what happened in my spirit. The responses I gave to Reverend Cary during confirmation classes, as we struggled to stay awake in his large-backed, fake leather chairs, came from my mind and not my heart. Prayer was when we informed God of our wishes. Communion meant remembering all Christ had sacrificed in order that we might be saved; it burdened us with the responsibility of living up to this gift.

The Bible was a teacher, but the Bible was problematic. We avoided the radical politics of the Israelites' flight from Egypt and Jesus' cavorting with lepers, and so missed out on our tradition's liberating message. The church Bible never became more than a storybook, wider than the spread of my ten-year-old fingers, pages gold-edged, with a smoky smell at the spine and a hundred and fifty years of hand grease at the corners. It sat on the lectern, far from my family's pew at center left, and didn't rank very high in my opinion as good reading material. Later on, when I began composing heartfelt poetry about Our Father and locking it in my journal for fear that anyone might discover I was *religious*, my sentiments had more to do with the church, which had inserted the Father-God into my imagination, than the winging spirit I spoke with at night.

I remember serving communion with Reverend Kindly. There were few kids in the congregation and even fewer willing to be acolytes, so fairly often I donned the off-white cotton robe in the musty back hall, securing it with a rope tied about my waist the way I imagined a monk might. We stood side by side, facing the congregation from on high, and read important words to the people. Then we turned our backs on them to kneel and read important words to the cross hanging in the alcove. Holding the cup, Reverend Kindly rocked back and forth on his heels, and I wondered if I should rock, too—if this was part of the ritual about which he'd neglected to tell me.

The stiff formality of the meal contained less hope for me than the pancake brunch the youth group served after church one year, rowdy with the expectation of traveling to Lancaster, Pennsylvania. When we made it there, caravanning across farmland in our mothers' station wagons, we eventually sat around a Mennonite family's breakfast table holding hands to bless that morning's milk, fresh eggs, and butter. Their plates were heavy ceramic and we drank juice from canning jars. For communion my church gave me the ritual and the real thing. But it neglected to name the ordinary meal holy.

I longed for the Mennonites' simple, God-centered life the same way I longed to be a monk. The graces my family spoke at home were rote. My mother's unwavering trust in a loving, divine presence surrounded our mealtimes like steam rising from the casseroles she prepared, but we were afraid to give this trust voice before each other or before God. If we colored outside the lines of a formulaic prayer, God would no longer keep his safe distance but might come spilling out of our hearts. Our unbounded potential would expose itself. This was too terrifying.

At church, Joys and Concerns presented the congregation with a similar dilemma. Joys and Concerns is that moment in most Methodist services when the congregation is invited to share prayers in order that we might uphold in spirit one another's struggles and celebrations during worship and throughout the week. Yet when the pastor asked the people what we wanted to lift before God, it was a rare Sunday when someone raised a hand and offered a prayer, usually for a dying aunt or friend with cancer. A dusty discomfort fell over us. As a child I sensed in that silence the heaviness of bit tongues and unintelligible aches. I did not understand how the dread secrets of our personal lives—lesbianism, unwed pregnancy, incest, prolonged clinical depression, drugs that, yes, even the youth group teens dabbled in—went unspoken because of even dreader rules—shame, guilt, the assumption that we were separate and alone in our suffering, the pretense that hard things shouldn't happen because our God is loving and Christ has already risen. Even pleasure and personal joy went undercover. Sex didn't exist. Accomplishments were shared only reluctantly for fear of sin's second name, which was pride. We shifted in our pews as the pastor grew impatient.

Looking back, I now know the unwritten rule of public worship in our congregation was *keep it clean*, don't allow the messiness of personal lives or corporate sin to smear the illusion of our normalcy. When one woman suffered an abusive marriage, she did so alone, and the congregation was cheated because the woman we thought we knew wasn't the complete picture—she was distorted, less than her full complexity. As a result, all of us sitting in those pews were two-dimensional. I felt the façade: My teenage sense of alienation wasn't welcome Sunday mornings, but there was plenty of room for my friendly, capable self.

God was flat for us as well, a socially acceptable God, a God present when things ran smoothly and absent in times of difficulty. God's enduring love wasn't very amazing because we couldn't look the world's injustice, that we helped perpetuate, in the face. As a congregation, we neglected to notice the privilege of our white skin (or Mr. Jones' isolation, the only black man in the congregation, hidden behind the organ console), our middle-class inertia, and our heterosexual family-centered notions of faith. Alongside goodness and kindness and inklings of justice, insidious prejudices sneaked into my belief system. To speak the truth about one life would break apart a safe knowing of God and the established order of our congregation's interactions; it would launch us into an abyss of unknowing, which is where God's creative work usually happens. None of us could risk it.

Within the last fifteen years, John Wesley's teaching about the quadrilateral has filtered down to the typical Methodist parishioner, radically changing how we can perceive God's involvement in the world. Wesley stated that a life of faith should be built equally upon tradition, scripture, reason and experience; in other words, religious heritage, sacred texts, careful thought and our everyday lives are all means by which God reveals Godself. When I was growing up, the last two possibilities never crossed my mind. Even within the Bible, my congregation avoided the wisdom texts of *Ecclesiastes* as skillfully as we skirted the erotica of the *Song of Songs*. These books were too effluent, too charged. Were someone to have asked me, *Who has the right to talk about God?*, the answer would have been ministers, always male, and the saintly authors of the Bible. There was no room for mystics, monastics, contemporary writers, God forbid the laity. The radical idea that our experiences might contain the handwriting of God never occurred to us. Because we couldn't call our chaotic potlucks, full of spaghetti casseroles and jello salads, a form of communion, communion itself was disassociated from the ordinary act of sharing a meal. An individual knowing of God, independent of religious ritual and the weekly lectionary, was inconceivable.

I think of myself, a five- then ten- then fifteen-year-old sitting in the pew, one day to discover herself a bisexual woman. Church gave me a lexicon and a mythology into whose stiff shoes I squeezed my conscious understanding of God. Later on, during my first Bible study at college, I suddenly understood what could be done with all the religious baggage that had accumulated in my head: I could *talk* about it, as my parents never did; I could debate theology like the academic discipline that it is. I mistook these lively discussions for a spiritual life. After a particularly heady debate one night, I walked back to my dorm room under the Minnesota winter sky, every star cold and sharp, and I questioned the very existence of God. The universe was vast and unfathomable. In my head I could work through the tenets of faith, but beneath the immense heavens I knew how disconnected this intellectual crafting was from the workings of my heart. I removed the monk's silver dove from around my neck and replaced it with a cross. The cross weighed more. Its sharp angles sometimes cut into the skin of my breasts. Inside, I felt very much alone.

Yet it always seemed to me that the church, more than any other place, had secret passages opening into mystery. During rehearsals for a youth-led worship service when I was fourteen, I made the dramatic gesture of a cross as I pronounced the benediction. Here was something mighty, holy, full of ritual. Afterward, my Sunday school teacher said that, really, gesturing was unnecessary; the words were enough. I flushed with embarrassment. I wanted to enter the world of faith as fully as Linny and I entered our fantasies, in high heels and white gloves. Ritual here came so close—the slippery choir robes we zipped with nervous fingers, the flame carried up to the altar to usher us into worship, the Lord's prayer we recited en masse, sharing intonations (a sibilant union of "trespasses as we forgive those who trespass against us"; breaths of expectation between "kingdom" and "power" and "glory, forever and ever"). On the one hand, I felt the church had no room for my contemplative, imaginative love affair with God. On the other, it shook the floorboards of my soul with the organ's postlude, jubilant and carousel-like—Widor's *Toccata*—and, while adults milled about, chatting, I danced down the aisle, my skirt flying and arms outstretched.

Marcy and I sang in the four-person choir, directed by Clarence Jones. He was a short, bearded man who had studied music at Oxford. I think he always regretted the dearth of boys' choirs in the states, because he trained us to sing sweetly and clearly, with British accents. Most often we sang in Latin. The round shapes of our vowels and the repetition of phrases that when spoken were flat and empty but when sung (*Hodie, nobis de ceilo pax vera descendit; Agnus Dei, qui tollis peccata mundi*) resonated with meaning, gave our worship a rare mystical dimension. Standing beside the organ console, just to the left of the altar, Mr. Jones would point to the farthest corner of the ceiling, across the sanctuary. "Send your voice there," he'd say. "Breathe from your abdomen, from way down *here*," and he'd clutch below his belt buckle. We sang not with our heads but from the center of our bodies. On Christmas Eve, we began our processional with the *a capella* soprano singing "Once in Royal David's City." Then our voices arched over the congregation; they filled rows of empty space with the pronouncement of birth. When the people and organ joined us for the third and remaining verses, the sanctuary was so full of song I knew, not in my head but in my singing spirit, how completely Christ feeleth for our sadness and shareth in our gladness.

And after the agony of Joys and Concerns in each service there was that moment called Passing of the Peace. Perhaps because our congregation was quickly dying off, with more than half of our membership over sixty years old, or perhaps because most of us had spent our lives worshipping within those walls, we couldn't limit ourselves to polite handshakes. We met one another with hugs, squeezed hands, and light kisses on the cheek. The pastor stood helplessly in the pulpit as his service fell to pieces of chaotic joy and concern— snatches of ambulance corps gossip, compliments on making the honor roll which had been printed in the local paper, the real news from Marian's hospital room that couldn't be shared publicly. There was community despite our stiff oak pews and the unspoken rules that prohibited intimacy in public prayer. We loved one another tangentially, with labor-of-love deviled eggs the old ladies brought to potlucks, with measures of Happy Birthday that Mr. Jones slipped into the Bach prelude. Out of financial desperation, we opened our church doors and welcomed other congregations to worship in our sanctuary—first an Episcopal church, and later an evangelical Hispanic church whose members greeted us on the sidewalk after our service holding Bibles, tambourines, and electric guitars. We became advocates for a small non-profit pastoral counseling center that rented space in the church basement. This was the faith that was lived, and it taught my heart more about God than any confirmation class or monotone sermon.

Spiritual connections were formed despite the silence and alienation—connections that endure the passage of time, work their transformation by splitting apart what oppresses us, and bind us together in our weakness. I held Mr. Jones' dark, articulate fingers and kissed his scratchy beard before he died. I send one church mother, who has since told me of her struggles with Dissociative Identity Disorder, drafts of this manuscript, and she sends back ten-page correspondences urging me on in my work of truth-telling. She assures me that our experiences are holy and worth naming as such. Back in the dirt-floor basement beneath the sanctuary, past the stacks of old pews and boxes of Sunday school coloring books, in the place where a single bare light bulb was turned on by pulling a knotted thread, there was a mammoth wooden Bible, perhaps four feet by six, painted with the words of Luke 2:10: "And the angel said unto them, Fear not . . . " As children we stole down there during advent to look with awe at this anomaly, this piece of ostentatious religious art that the grown-ups made certain would never see daylight. We felt its dark plight should be redeemed, and so we screamed Luke's message from the basement; we shouted it in hopes that the whole neighborhood would hear: "For behold, I bring you glad tidings of great joy, which shall be for all the people. For unto you is born this day, in the city of David, a Savior, which is Christ the Lord!" We stomped the earth and raised billows of dust. And so beneath the layers of church teaching, beneath a lulling language of formula and familiarity, beneath doctrine, hierarchy, and inertia; beneath all the heaviness of silence and hurt lies this bare experience which is a collective shout of joy. Inasmuch as we become a community of love growing in love, we are also the body of Christ. This is the God I am learning to worship.

I keep a photograph on my writing desk. In it I am four years old. I'm wearing a pastel green dress my mother made, with smocking across the front. The hem falls just above my knees, which are still chubby with baby fat. A purple sweater my grandmother knit for me is slipping off my shoulders. I am standing at the top of two slab steps, holding open with both arms the swinging doors of a garden gate. Above me the trees are overexposed with sunlight, and over my right shoulder, half hidden by the gate, is my mother.

We were in Williamsburg on one of our hundreds of road trips. My father worked as a lawyer for IBM, which he told me stood for "I've been moved"; it meant we moved five times before I was seven years old, and always had the financial wherewithal to travel for pleasure. When we moved from Potomac, Maryland, to La Cañada, California, we took a month to drive there. My grandmother packed a surprise box that took up half our trunk space, from which Marcy and I pulled a single present daily—a small box of raisins, a deck of cards, a rubber man who could twist his legs around his neck. When Marcy and I fought over seat space, my father brought out a piece of plywood to fit between the front armrest and back seat. For a while it separated us, but then became a puppet show stage. Every evening the family sat together on a soft motel bed and narrated the day's moose sightings and picnic adventures into a tape recorder. This, at age five and then again at seven, when we drove back, was the first journal I ever kept: familial, united, full of laughter and my parents' gentle coaxing.

It was my father who imbued us with wanderlust. He was happiest behind the wheel, his right hand idling on the shift, his left arm growing dark at the open window. Marcy and I caught his spirit of adventure; despite my mother's protests, we cheered him on every time he suggested, "How about a little detour?" We detoured up a snow-covered Rocky Mountain pass in search of a hot spring, and wound up stuck in a snow bank, trying to put chains on the tires. Once, driving in Italy, we detoured up a Tuscan dirt road so narrow we couldn't turn around for fifteen miles. We dead-ended high in the mountains at a cluster of five houses where chickens were strutting in the dust, and every door opened to see who in heaven's name had arrived. I felt at once my mother's intense embarrassment at invading their privacy and my father's elation at discovering this spot, not even on the map. From my father we got the sense that whatever lurked beyond the next bend in the road—a desert vista, an anomalous twenty-one thousand pound ball of twine, the sulfur smell of a spa town—might enlighten us, might bring us to a new and dangerous awareness.

Every noon, just as we were growing hungry, my father began a quest for the perfect picnic spot. Under ideal conditions, perfect meant sunny, isolated from people and the trashy evidence of people, with a good view. The quest would take hours, my mother's demands that we stop becoming more adamant as my sister's and my whining grew louder. But usually he found it. Suddenly he'd swing the Dodge onto the shoulder, spitting gravel, and point to a boulder at the edge of a stream. "That's it!" he'd pronounce. The family, relieved, spread out the moth-eaten army blanket and unscrewed jars of peanut butter and jelly. What Marcy and I only sensed, kicking our ankles in the water after lunch, cupping our hands in the eddies to catch minnows, chasing each other over the rocks, my father knew—that beauty nourishes as well as food, and where we place ourselves is of infinite importance.

Which is why I keep this photograph on my desk. In it, as a child, I have placed myself at the open gate. My mouth is wide and my face expectant. I am looking at my father who is taking the picture. Ten steps behind my right shoulder my mother is approaching me, her hair still long and face attentive. Both my arms are outstretched in order to hold wide the swinging doors. It seems as though the world I am entering is magnificent. How could it not be? Ivy spills over the brick walls, the steps lead down to adventure, and my parents are behind and before me. My father never spoke of God, but he had this for faith: There are places God meant for us to find, and we must journey until we come to them.

The place I came to love more than any other was Tarrytown, setting for Washington Irving's "Legend of Sleepy Hollow," "overlooking the majestic Hudson River Valley," as my junior high principal reminded us each morning over the P.A. The Tappan Zee bridge sets one foot in Tarrytown and the other in Nyack, two and a half miles across the river. At that point the river is still estuarial, the flow tides hauling in seaweed and the salt smell of the ocean, the ebb tides carrying down fresh water from Tear of the Clouds in the Adirondacks. There are always seagulls overhead. On the west bank across from Tarrytown are the Palisades, steep columnar basalt cliffs falling into the river. When a college admissions interviewer asked my sister what she considered to be a unique strength of her high school, Marcy replied, "The view."

We made our final move from California to New York when I was seven, my father scouting ahead to buy the house. He brought back five blurry black and white photographs that made the split-level, 1950's house seem like a mausoleum. My mother cried for weeks. Now she laughs—she should have known better; she should have trusted my father's sense of placement and need for beauty.

The house was, indeed, dull and suburban, but it was dominated by windows facing the river. The view erased the house. From the living room, we looked across a lawn canopied by two-hundred-year-old hemlocks, an oak even older, and upstart tulip poplars I could not put my arms around. At the far edge the lawn sloped suddenly down to a swamp and railroad tracks. When a train went by, the swamp-grass tossed its hair in the wind. The river came right up to the rails, and in stormy weather geysers of spray crashed on the rocks and flooded the tracks. I sat in the living room rocker, drinking in the view. Occasionally the Clearwater, a reconstructed Hudson River sloop, would tack past the house with sails unfurled, throwing spray over the ship rails. I squinted then, blurring the railroad tracks and telephone wires, and saw the Hudson Valley as it looked to the Dutch colonialists who originally settled our sleepy town.

The river was my family's excuse to sit and stare into space, to be idle, to observe, to be absorbed by beauty. It was my meditation. I became all eyes and allowed something magnificently larger than myself to fill my being. If anything taught me the nature of God, it was the landscape of my childhood. It imprinted itself on my person; it yanked at my heart until I loved it best.

All summer long Marcy and I swam in that dirty river. Marcy dog-paddled, her short black hair plastered to her face, and she did dolphin dives close to shore. I swam laps around the two rafts, back stroke and crawl. If, on a sunny day, we dove deep and opened our eyes under water, we each independently discovered how every refracted beam of light converged on us. Sometimes I slipped off the top of my bathing suit to see what the Hudson felt like on my bare chest. It was slippery and cool, and, when I was older, made my breasts alert. Emerging from the river when we were little, we washed oil mustaches from our faces. After the environmental groups had done their work and the water was clean again, we left the Hudson's musty salt to dry on our skin.

From the river I learned my north and south. I learned that the cycle of tides pushes water upstream even when the end destination is the heaving, mighty ocean. The river was my wide margin, my breathing space, on the page the left-hand line against which my childhood was written. It was my first conscious image of God sprung completely from my own experience and not from a Sunday school book.

One evening when I was in high school, I draped a towel over my shoulders and rode my bike down to the beach. The beach club was empty except for a few men puttering on their sailboats, to which they rowed on a leaky dinghy. I slipped out of my tennis shoes and placed them, with the towel, on the retaining wall. The sand sank under my heels. A border of seaweed shifted in unison at the water's edge, its succulent, bulbous tendrils reaching and retreating, reaching and retreating.

I stepped over the weeds and into the water, where pebbles and flecks of mica bit at my feet. Waves washed in, the water rising to my knees. I walked until the sand gave way to muck, and then I pushed off, a dolphin dive. The rhythm of my breast stroke alternated with the rise and fall of the waves. There was a floating rope that cordoned off the swimming area, beyond which we were not allowed to go—with good reason, as the area was large and deep enough, protected by the breakwater from fierce undertows and the current. But the lifeguards quit at five o'clock. I swam beyond the last raft and ducked under the weedy cord.

The water smelled clean, an ebb tide, less heavy and salty than when it rushed up from the Atlantic. I swam directly west toward the Palisades, toward the widening sun and cumulus dyed red. Once I passed the tip of the beach's peninsula, the current heaved at me until I turned north, exchanging the breast stroke for the crawl in order not to be swept away. The shores rose on either side of me like the thighs of a woman giving birth. I was immersed in the rush of water on a journey, water determined to reach its home. I had to labor upriver to stay in one place.

The Hudson was a lover kissing every pore of my nearly naked body. If God was like the river, then I was in dynamic relationship with God; we touched one another, we moved one another, and something was born of that contact. I flipped to my back because I was tired. The sun reached the lip of the cliffs and flattened like an egg yolk. Suddenly the water was black and I had to turn back before the air grew dark as well. I rolled in on the swells. At the beach, sand stuck to my ankles. My skin smelled briny and green. Huddled under the towel, I watched the sun sketch its bright signature. God was everything, I decided—the mountain water, the river's journey, the steep-banked shores, the spilling sea. The backwash was God and the still moment at the changing tide was God. I would leave Tarrytown and the valley and New York, but the river would always be home, home carved like a riverbed into my body. My blood was really river water and in me was that drive to reach the sea.

When I was very little, I had a dream. In the dream I swim under water that is clear and brightened by a blue sky. Tired, I finally reach an island of white sand, where great festivities are about to take place. All the children have created Lego structures and ornate floats and are lining up to parade into the cathedral. A round woman from church explains to me that these are their offerings. "What will you bring?" she asks me. All I have is a thermos of lemonade strapped to my waist. I march at the back of the parade feeling sad and lonely that I have so little to give God. When I come to the cathedral door, adults are waiting there with a wreath of lit candles. They pity me, and place it on my head. I no longer have the lemonade.

Inside, the space is dark and enormous. I sense crowds but the only thing visible at the end of the line of children is the altar, lit and piled high with gifts. My empty hands make me nervous. What will I offer God once I climb those steps? Everything in my mind is a whirlwind, so that I am singing before I know it. Barefoot, I climb the steps to the altar singing music I have never heard before, which comes directly from my heart. My song rises sweetly to the far dark corners of the sanctuary. I feel the people hold their breath. Then I die.

Everything I do today is about learning to sing that spontaneous song. I knew it better as a child, spinning wildly on the tire swing digging my feet into the earth, than I know it now, and so I write these memories in hopes of again hearing its melody. God is so profoundly incarnate that we learn of God mostly through a mother holding us to her breast, or through a community's *Gloria Patri*, or through a place that laps at our soul. What would I call Spirit if my father hadn't danced me to bed, singing "Rock Around the Clock," or if my mother hadn't conversed with me as she tucked me in, calling it prayer? What would I know of divine relationship without my sister, pouting then giggling as we pumped the swings to the highest point then kicked off our shoes, sending them whirling through the air? I name these experiences blessed.

But when the retreat center's garage fire burned up my silver dove necklace, the symbol of my childhood faith, I had not worn it in over a decade. Something had gone awry in the intervening years; something had been denied. My aunt sent a replacement pendant made by the hands of a Weston Priory monk, and I wear it overtly now, bouncing on my shirt, with the prayer that I might uncover what separated me from the undaunted, imaginative girl who used to clutch its cold silver in the middle of a dream-filled night. Somehow I suspect that this is what coming to understand and name my body bisexual is really about. My journey points back toward that childish, open heart, which didn't know better than to believe that spirit was solid and tangible. Now I learn to listen to that little girl. Now I ask her, as no one ever did, to sing to me what she knows of God.

Unlocking the Garden

Mistress Mary stood up and looked at it with an almost frightened face as it hung from her finger.

"Perhaps it has been buried for ten years," she said in a whisper. "Perhaps it is the key to the garden!"

One afternoon when I was still teaching and struggling with questions about my sexual identity, I lay down on my bedroom floor, exhausted from a day at school, to watch the sun angle steeply between two apartment buildings and alight on the window sill. Dust floated there, wraithlike. Breath filled my chest and then released itself, my back sinking to the floor. Then, suddenly, I sat bolt upright. Another dusty beam of light, this one streaming past the joist of a barn loft, had appeared in my memory. I hastily pulled a folder of my early writing from the bookshelf.

Shoved between pages of angst-ridden adolescent poetry and English essays was a story called "Mistress of Her Choice." The pages were yellowed, with my tenth grade teacher's red pen-marks in the margins. I remembered taking the title from *Hamlet*; the mistress was Hamlet's soul, choosing to cleave good Horatio to itself in friendship. I couldn't remember my own story's plot. Still, I knew with conviction that this piece, written when I was sixteen with all its teenage limitations in style and form, was the last piece of writing I'd put my heart into. It was the key I'd wanted, the Elgin marble that would explain why I'd cut out my childhood self and cast it away. I began to read with trepidation, as though the words had come from someplace other than inside myself.

Morgan and Elaine are teenage cousins, visiting for the first time after many years' separation. They escape the formal chatter of their parents and dash out to the old barn, the play-place of their childhood. Morgan runs barefoot, confident of her steps because this is her home. Elaine tosses her blond hair behind her and is careful not to get mud on her fashionable shoes. The two girls had spent their growing years engrossed in a make-believe drama that they enacted in a forgotten room of the barn loft. They had rummaged through a box of their mothers' bridesmaid and prom dresses and padded lightly over the hay-strewn floor wearing old ballet slippers. Each scene of their fantasy had begun with a ritual: When they slid their fingers into the slender cotton of their mothers' faded white gloves, Morgan and Elaine slipped into their imaginary roles and didn't emerge until their hands were bared. The plot of "The Great Play," as they called it, had been full of stymied romance. There was an imaginary evil duke who had matted dark hair and beady eyes, who always managed to thwart the girls' budding relationships with other, more dashing, imaginary men. He was keenly aware of how close the two women were. Finally he devised a way to trap them. With his magical powers, he inflicted Elaine with a fatal disease and then used his ability to heal her as a bribe to convince Morgan to marry him. In order to save her friend's life, Morgan would have to sacrifice her own to a destructive marriage.

But in midsummer, just as their drama had reached its climax, Elaine's parents interrupted it abruptly by moving her family to the city. Over the intervening years, on busy streets and in coffee houses, Elaine had become sophisticated. She had turned her back on the world of make-believe and had grown up. Morgan, with long black hair and brooding eyes, stayed in the small farming town and refused, even as a teenager, to wear lipstick.

This is the cousins' first visit, six years after Elaine's move. When the girls reach the stairway at the back of the barn, its steps are rotted. They balance their way up and across the few support beams remaining to reach their special room. The air is dusty. There is one empty window frame looking across the yard to the farmhouse. Dirty but untouched, the props of their fantasy world lie folded in a box just as they had left them.

Morgan holds her mother's faded wedding dress up to Elaine and they laugh—it is pinned up to her knees. They reminisce for a while, the way adolescents do; childhood was golden and limitless and shattered abruptly. They piece together the story, recalling where it had been cut off. They blame Elaine's parents for its lack of resolution. For fun they try on their old costumes, recounting the build-up of tension as they remove pins from the skirt-hems. Morgan is exuberant; she enters her role as swiftly as she dons the white gloves. Elaine, brushing blond curls from her face, glances out the window as though someone might be watching.

The girls enact the climax. Elaine wakes up from her sickbed. She is in awe of being alive; for her sake, Morgan has agreed to marry the duke, who will surely beat her as he has his past three wives.

"How can I repay you?" Elaine asks. "You, who have sacrificed your happiness for me—what can I do?" Morgan is silent for a moment, and then requests Elaine's sworn and devoted friendship. Elaine is willing enough to agree until Morgan falls to her knees, demanding that such a promise be sealed with a kiss.

A shocked pause fills the room. A kiss confuses the boundaries between make-believe and reality, a boundary that didn't exist when they were young.

> Elaine bent down to Morgan's sharp black eyes. She had forgotten how to kiss like a child kisses, without thinking, as she had when the wedding gown was pinned up and the ballet slippers were on her feet. It frightened her and she hesitated, attempting to tear her mind away from this interwoven plot of her childhood. She was confused and suddenly ill at ease, not knowing whether to view the situation from a child's or an adult's eyes.
>
> Rapidly, Elaine turned away from Morgan's close and passionate face, and leaned out the window, her back to the room. The air was heavy with ozone, and the horizon of fields past the trees at the creek was hazy. She breathed deeply, but there was no refreshment in the summer humidity. She could not concentrate.

Elaine longs to seal that commitment, but cannot—not now, not as a self-conscious teenager. She leaves Morgan, angry and betrayed, on her knees, and steps out onto the exposed beams of the loft. "She felt years of dirt on her bare feet," my high-school self wrote, "and knew she could never return to this small haven again. Far, far down lay the flat tractor tires, rotten four-by-fours, and rusted bicycles; she was a lofty white creature high up in the clouds of dust and woodwork."

I held typing paper between my fingers, but it seemed I had just woken from a dream. "Mistress of Her Choice" was heavy with my adolescent longings and deep-rooted fears; its meaning was layered because every image represented a part of me at the moment I wrote it. I was both little girls who knew their fantasy world was also the real world, and who were unafraid to kiss. I was the older Morgan, straining to believe it is possible to carry the whole of her ardent, sensual self into adulthood. I was Elaine, torn from her most intimate friend by social pressures and because she distrusts her instinct—that the love of a woman is good. I was the kiss, at the same time romantic and not, representing commitment to another woman and a willingness to thrust oneself into a place where one is no longer in control. I was the comment in the margin written by my teacher, Mr. Fellows —"the kiss is a bit too much"—and the rampant homophobia I learned like a spelling correction. And in me was the distance from the high, dusty loft-beams to the trash-strewn barn floor, the separation between what we envision the world could be and what it is.

When I was sixteen I became the mistress of my choice, wandering the public school halls in a skirt and blouse, hair braided and pinned up like a nun. Mr. Fellows stood at the end of the shop corridor in khaki pants and a red vest, his hands on his hips. He watched me approach. He marked the air with his sharp gaze the same way he splattered red ink across my short stories. I carried my shoulders stiffly and slapped the heels of my sandals against the tiles. "You have the most peculiar walk," he said when I met up with him. When I think of myself at sixteen, I look through my English teacher's critical eyes and see the gay gait, hip swing and books clutched close to my chest. I see a girl on a precipice. The angle of her chin distances her from intimacy, and her hunched posture protects and then represses the daring, fantastic woman inside. Under the watchful eyes of a man, I walked away from my truth into the body that women are expected to wear. To Mr. Fellows I said, smiling, "It's the walk of a writer." The swish and flair of my skirt was a stride to which artists are entitled. But with every echoing step down that corridor I constrained my gait and shoved its creativity into nerves and stilted angles. When I disallowed the vessel of my body to be itself, the God who resided there moved elsewhere, up into my head. I learned the walk of denial.

And so the yellowed sheets of paper, typewritten my sophomore year of high school, contained the last honest story I ever told. In the years between writing "Mistress of Her Choice" and that exhausted afternoon when I found it again, tucked in my bookshelf, I had not written a successful piece of prose. Stories began with a main character's unfocused longing and never found language to name what was missing or the propulsion of plot to fill it. Essays avoided first person singular pronouns and took on the disembodied voice my teachers expected. I put energy into poetry instead, where a lyric moment can stand on its own without explanation. I called myself a writer, but most of my real work stayed hidden between the covers of journals. Creative energy springs from knowing that one's longings are spirit-driven; mine was crumpled in a rotting cardboard box. I locked away my ardent self, the part that loves women as well as men and believes there can be a continuum between childhood fantasy and the world as adults construct it. I left this creative source, locked and inaccessible, in the lofty recesses of my imagination.

Dormancy

"There's lots o' dead wood as ought to be cut out," he said.
"An' there's a lot o' old wood, but it made some new last year.
This here's a new bit," and he touched a shoot which looked
brownish green instead of hard, dry grey.

   Mary touched it herself in an eager, reverent way.

   "That one?" she said. "Is that one quite alive—quite?"

   Dicken curved his wide smiling mouth.

   "It's as wick as you or me," he said.

Dormancy: the state of being alive but not actively growing.
Gregory of Nyssa, a first century Christian ascetic, called sin
the failure to grow. I have understood sin to be separation
from God, but I now know both definitions are the same.
In my adolescence, I thought myself asexual and in my
young adulthood heterosexual, and both misnamings in-
hibited my multifaceted passion. My word and its story
remained dormant. For years I avoided growing, and so
hindered God's continuing creation. In thought and word
and deed, oh God, I confess.

Surely there are reasons a girl removes her mind from her
body and forces her spirit underground. Who, for instance,
tells eleven-year-old girls that their bodies, in their awkward

metamorphoses, are evidence of God's unfolding self manifest in our flesh? Who tells them that loving their bodies shows reverence for their creator? In good conditions a silence surrounds our bodily transformations and cuts off the critical flow of oxygen. But when our bodies don't follow the rules, pubic hair emerging past the border of a bathing suit, or breasts a bit too large, or eyes roaming to the dark-haired girl in the back of the classroom instead of to everyone's blond sweetheart, the message is clear: Our bodies violate what is clean and normal; they forsake the billboard images and the boys' locker room expectations and are an offense to society. Then God is distant. Young girls cry into their pillows at night. We diet and shave. We spend our lives rectifying the apparent wrong done to us by our bodies. Surely this lumpy flesh won't represent *me* in the world. Surely my true self is more beautiful than *this*.

Adolescence was for me a time of shutting down key passages between my body and the thinking, dreaming, praying parts of myself. I didn't want to be conscious of the frightening sensations that caused me to fall in love with clearly the wrong people. I knew what it meant to be normal, to jump excitedly to the beat of music, to want very badly to slip into the seat of the bus beside Antonio with his floppy head of hair. But my body betrayed me. It grew too fast for my clothes. It lost its grace. It wanted other things, too, like to hold my best friend's hand as we walked along the Hudson's breakwaters. And what was normal betrayed me by changing as quickly as the latest style of designer jeans. I couldn't even register all the social expectations for my body, much less live up to them: Stay thin, stay fit, toss your shiny hair, be smart but appear stupid, flirt with boys but don't get into trouble, by all means be beautiful. Even my mother sent me mixed messages. Out of her longing she said, "Be your own person; never mind what others think." Out of her fear she watched carefully how much I ate and fretted over my social ineptitude. How could I possibly reconcile my body, growing more gawky and humiliating each day, with what I was taught to believe—that God created man and woman and called them good? My spiritual life dissociated itself from what was physical. I learned to view my body from a critical distance. Straight hair hung in my eyes, hips ballooned outward, and my skin was pocked with pimples. Dormancy is living ten years without seeing beauty in my body.

The last time I touched myself kindly as a child was one spring night when I was eleven. The windows were open and the street lamp, overgrown with bittersweet, cast dim shadows across the wall. Looking up at the curtains drifting idly above my bed, I remembered how at recess I had spun, as I often did, headfirst around the iron railing that separated our paved playground from the town sidewalk. This time it hurt my chest. I was afraid something was wrong. Maybe there were gaping sores on my chest, or maybe I had some rare disease that could keep me in bed for months. Cautiously I ran my hand under the sheets up my front and found two tender lumps in what had always been muscle and bone. Suddenly I knew. "They feel like mini-hotdogs," I remember thinking. I was mildly disgusted. Had they been sores I could have at least told someone.

Instead I ignored the changes and touched my body only with the practical, course sweep of the washcloth in my morning shower. I understood that my body-self should be stopped up and held secret, just as my mother showed me, straddled over the toilet seat when I bled for the first time. She was gentle in her explanation; she bought me pads and stored them in the bathroom Marcy and I shared. But somehow, now, a rift appeared between us. Our bodies were separate; the blood made it clear that I existed outside my mother, with my own cycles, my own privacies. I could no longer walk with ease out of the shower while she was in the room. When we looked into one another's eyes we knew less than we did before. When I was crippled over with cramps, my mother put her hand on my shoulder but couldn't touch the world of pain inside.

Womanhood for me was about covering up the messiness we were given, the hair, the blemishes, the breasts, the blood. "Why doesn't Elizabeth wear a bra?" Muffy Farrell, tossing her curls, asked Julie during seventh grade science lab. Julie grabbed my elbow and dragged me into the supply room. We took Bunsen burners from the dirty shelves and Julie passed on the question. Muffy got what she wanted: I spent a miserable afternoon with my mother in Howland's dressing room praying incessantly that no one I knew would walk by. The dangling bits of white fabric my mother handed to me each felt like an insult. Had I been able to look my mother in the face I would have found compassion there. The next day in the girls' locker room I no longer had to turn my back to the others when I slipped out of my gym shirt. But I did anyhow. In health class we asked questions about sex on anonymous slips of paper so that when the teacher pulled them from the box and read them aloud and the classroom burst out laughing, no one had to know who had written them. Except that eventually we all stopped asking questions. I became resigned. The first time I shaved my legs I cried and cried into the shower's steam. Beloved bits of my body washed down the drain. No one else ever knew.

Of course these little things—bodily, ordinary details—rarely appeared on the pages of my junior high journals. I didn't record the first day of my period, the day I became a woman, capable of birthing new life. I didn't write down the small romantic crushes I endured in silence, or the disarming moments of physical attraction. I had *ideas*, and it was clear to me that the life of the mind was nobler and more transcendent. I filled pages with discoveries I'd made: the similarity between the spinning of atoms and the orbit of planets; how everyone at school seemed to be acting out a drama. The mind, I came to believe, was the seat of creativity, and the best way to comprehend mystery was through exercising the intellect. School encouraged me: I grew studious. Church confirmed my suspicions by neglecting to ever mention that its congregation had bodies. Physical sensation never formed itself into words—in my mind, mouth or on the page—and so it didn't exist.

Sexual sensation especially didn't exist. If my peers claimed it did by erasing hearts into the colored covers of their spiral notebooks and by wearing hickeys the way some women do wedding rings, I scorned their version of love. Part of my haughtiness was a defense mechanism, because I was smart and an outcast and intuited that any boy I might set my eyes on would reject me. When Mr. Cappella forgot how to bisect an angle with the wooden chalkboard compass during a lesson, and I put down my copy of *The Once and Future King* in order to show him, I forfeited any slim chance

I had at appearing attractive to my classmates. Since I had nothing to lose, I figured boys would have to take me *as is*, should one ever deem to do so. I wore what I wanted to wear. One day I wore a blue shirt my mother had embroidered for my father in the seventies; the front was covered with symbols of his life (the legal scale, hot peppers, an airplane, his daughters' tricycle) and across the shoulders of the back were the flowers of his garden. My three friends thought it was cool; everyone else treated me like I was off my rocker. This was hard work for a twelve-year-old. The social expectations of our gender are never clearer than in a junior high hallway.

But I also grew aloof, I now suspect, because I was waiting to feel sexual the way others described it. I'd been waiting since Julie first showed me a photograph of Sting and asked, "Isn't he *sweet*?" Notes, passed under the desk asking me to rank Clarence Fulton (blond, on the tennis team) and Terry Jones (olive-skinned, the class clown) on a scale of one to ten, baffled me. In my mind I called my friends' crushes superficial and their ranking systems punitive, but underneath they made me envious for some manner of feeling I apparently did not have. When I looked at Clarence his skin shone and his eyes were sharp; when I watched Terry, he made me laugh. But neither one moved me. I waited for monosexual attraction, for sheer physical desire for a boy simply because he was a boy, from seventh grade through college. I studied the patterns of relationship among my peers and learned them like a math lesson, a rote formula, ignorant of its inner workings.

Yet all along I knew desire. There were precious few people in my world with romantic or poetic sensibilities, so that when I met a rare kindred spirit I fell in love. It wasn't sexual love, I was quick to tell myself—that was something else; that was lusting after Sting's photograph. This love, I was convinced, was on a higher plane and didn't include the baseness of bodies. Merrill Kapron was a dark, whimsical girl in my after-school drawing class. I was eleven; she was ten and brilliant. When we gathered in a circle on the floor to share our sketchbooks, I sat near her. She opened her pages to a drawing of a horse whose galloping body was made up of tiny, intricate horses. I imagined her pencil moving in small curves, her back bent for hours in concentration. I wanted to race inside Merrill's imagination like one of her horses, mane and tail flying. She lent me her sketchbook and I read it cover to cover, pretending it was written for me. "Teach me to love," she scrawled under a sketch of gnarled oak trees; "Be there." The dreams she recorded in her fifth grade script seemed mystical. She was small, a black-eyed fairy, the first person I fell in love with.

The second was my seventh-grade English teacher, Mr. Polliche. He had laughing, hazel eyes and hands large enough to completely encompass mine, not that they ever did. He taught Kurt Vonnegut's "Harrison Bergeron" from the Great Books series, showing me for the first time as I whirled free of gravity with Harrison that a story can have multiple layers of meaning. Because of this, I disclosed to Mr. Polliche before anyone else what I then considered my deepest, darkest secret—that I wrote poetry. It took tremendous courage. I agonized over the essay, trying to describe how thoughts flew out in verse, how words fell into form and said for me on the page what was most true. I was a nervous schoolgirl waiting for his response. He was cavalier:

He gave it an A-minus. A twelve-year-old's soul seems deceptively small. But one time he looked at me across the room of squirrelly kids and our eyes locked. Mr. Polliche smiled warmly. Perhaps it was the bit of black cord exposed at my neck, I thought, or the weightless, dancing spirit between the lines of poetry I handed him. I was convinced he recognized the real me beneath the shy demeanor, and I loved him for it.

I knew passion and I knew physical attraction, but they were sparked seemingly at random by boys and girls. I walked from class to class down gender-erotic hallways feeling somehow handicapped—blind to the color everyone else saw so vividly, deaf to the mating calls. "I could not be as others were," I memorized from Edgar Allen Poe; "I could not see as others saw; / I could not bring my passions from a common spring." When I left Mr. Polliche for the wilderness of eighth grade, I plummeted into depression. I read Conrad's *Heart of Darkness* and found its black jungles familiar. "I have a foreign love," I wrote in my little pink poet's notebook as I knelt at my locker, holding back tears. I wrote it without knowing what I meant. Elbowing my way from music to English, English to science, a voice in my head (not dissimilar from other teenagers' insecurities, but seeming particular, seeming isolated) became persistent. "This isn't me," it repeated. "This isn't me, this isn't me." At first it was reassuring. I was more than the awkward bookworm others saw. Over the years, though, its volume increased until it blocked out other sounds. Only with hindsight do I read it as a warning signal. *Beware!* it says. *God-given essentials denied.* Today, when I hear "This isn't me," my heart races the way it did in junior high and I cut out, I escape whatever walls surround me to suck in great gasps of cold, fresh air.

The year Andrew Wyeth unveiled his Helga collection, I was magnatized by the single, contemplative portrait *Time* magazine offered and dragged my parents to the Brooklyn Museum exhibit. I spent hours glued to those New England portraits: Helga with her unruly hair coming out of pigtails. Helga leaning against the budding tree. Helga standing alone in the snow of a Vermont winter. Her posture told me there were worlds inside her just as lush and barren, just as wildly landscaped, as those in which Wyeth placed her. The excitement I felt was surely the same Julie felt fingering her photograph of Sting, but how could I have recognized it? My parents had to coax me through the special exhibit's glass doors and back into the heat of the city.

When I happened upon my ninth-grade English teacher, Mrs. Simion, standing in the hallway gazing out the big picture windows down over Tarrytown to the river—when I stumbled into her moment of silence in the hectic school day and found her connected to something (beauty? mystery? the heartbeat of the Hudson?) beyond the ordinary, of course I fell in love. I was on the lookout for that reflective pose—Helga's stance. I did my entire senior thesis on the epiphanal moment in James Joyce's *Portrait of the Artist as a Young Man* when Stephan Dedalus, "near to the wild heart of life," gazes across the strand to a young girl, "alone and still," who embodies his ecstasy. I can't remember now if I longed more for Dedalus, swept away in the fervor of his growth, or for the girl in her profound moment of quiet. I suspect I ached for both. They symbolized an erotic connection to the pulse of life, a connection that could span even the distance of a shoreline.

There was more than intellectual romanticism in my feelings for Mrs. Simion, however. For an entire summer she appeared cool and detached in my dreams, which in turn haunted my journal. "My consistently recurring dreams of Mrs. Simion puzzle and confuse me," I wrote at age sixteen. "I would like to believe that a part of my attraction is subconscious, unknown and unexplainable. . . . The other part is conscious—a recognized longing . . . to be respected for my true self, as I am by no one. I am fully aware that this idea is so far fetched, comprised mostly of hope and dreams. It is when I see how foolish it is that I turn to other explanations." Finally I "convicted myself" of homosexuality. "Which in itself is ludicrous. I have no physical longing for Mrs. Simion." I knew full well I wasn't aberrant; after all, I came from a good family and sometimes was attracted to boys. Yet I remember vividly the straight cut of Mrs. Simion's back as she sat on her desk to teach us, and the playful way she removed the heels of her feet from Italian shoes. I remember the fine curve of her ankle. Her classroom presence was exciting; I remember the word *ephemeral* because it was on our vocabulary list, and she told us Ben Franklin had written to a lover that their weekend together was "as ephemeral as the flutter of a butterfly's wing." So were the forty-four minutes I spent in her classroom each day.

"I wish I could make a bust of Mrs. Simion," I confessed to Dawn after school one day as we waited for the bus to our sculpture class at SUNY Purchase. Dawn looked at me strangely. Immediately I was embarrassed: I meant a bust of the head, I explained, not a bust-bust. The expression on

66

Dawn's face implied that I was weird beyond words. At that time I was absorbed in how sensual it is to create a form out of clay, how the tendons and muscles of the medium emerge between your fingers. Erik, the sculptor who taught us, eyed my work quizzically. He measured its straining sinews and thrusting angles against my quiet, conservative demeanor, the skirt and blouse beneath my canvas apron, the hair pinned in a bun. "It's very phallic, you know," he said to me. I shrugged. That night, when I found "phallic" in the dictionary, I decided it was an artist's prerogative. My sculptures grew even more animated and daring. I made voluptuous, eight-foot tall plaster pieces which my parents put in the back yard far enough out of sight that the neighbors wouldn't complain. I learned to pour bronze, and the red bubbling metal was for me original matter, the stuff of passion that formed the world.

I have only one memory, of all my growing years, that reveals my parents' awareness of non-heterosexual relationships. It was a sunny afternoon in my mother's kitchen. My mother commented on the comings and goings of our neighbors as she wiped plates from the dishwasher and stacked them in the cupboard. Across the street from us was an old brick colonial where two women in their mid-sixties gardened ceaselessly, their plantain lillies and cascading English ivy the envy of the block. As I walked to the bus stop each morning, they waved to me with their floral printed gloves. Dorothy Zalar had been a New York City librarian. She still wrote reviews of Hudson Valley history books for the local paper, was active in the American Association of University Women, and wore a wide-brimmed hat when she drove her bronze Chevy. Roseann was quiet, did the housework, and raised violets. To my parents' amusement, my sister and I referred to them as the Zalars. We didn't know Roseann's last name.

Around the corner was a cedar-shingled contemporary house with skylights, owned by a professional chef and, on Wednesday and Thursday mornings, a volunteer for Meals on Wheels. He was gregarious, the kind of man who offered me a handshake even when I was a kid and was unembarrassed to talk to his cat in front of others. Mostly we saw him steering his silver hatchback down the street towards town. When he had company, they were men.

The small comment my mother made, wiping a dish dry and shaking her head at Mr. Fortuno's bumper, was: "Well, we're surrounded by them."

My head snapped up. "Them, who?"

My mother hesitated, as though she'd stumbled into a minefield. But then she said it. "Homosexuals." It was the first time I'd heard that word from her.

I was shocked. I never thought of the Zalars as being "them"; they were just two old ladies living together. It was scandalous to me that "they"—the men around the corner— might be doing something other than inventing new recipes or trying to teach the cat tricks in "their" sunny attic. Every Christmas Eve my mother frosted loaves of *kuken,* wrapped them in cellophane, and sent us traipsing up the street in our red turtlenecks to deliver greetings to "them." Marcy and I sat politely while my father carried the conversation, the same as in every house on our block. What bearing, then, did this new information have? I sensed it was better not to ask.

Sometime during my junior year I bought a silk-screened tee-shirt. On the front was an icon: King Arthur, lying dead in Guinevere's embrace beneath a field of night sky. He was belted and crowned with gold. The barge they were on was drifting toward Avalon, and beneath the water were printed the final verses of Tennyson's *Idylls of the King*:

> Down that long water opening on the deep
> Somewhere far off, pass on and on, and go
> From less to less and vanish into light.

I was still crazy about King Arthur, but it was no longer a grade school enchantment with castles and knights. Now I was intrigued by how the same story could be told in a hundred different versions, how generations of storytellers had turned Merlin and Arthur into mythological figures. I loved Arthur's egalitarian table and the committed fervor of his knights' quest for the holy grail. I respected the way Arthur reconciled Christianity with the Druidic religion. I justified my interest in his romantic affairs with the wonderful ethical dilemma they presented. In the versions I liked best, Arthur's downfall is the result of a love triangle with Lancelot and Guinevere; several stories have them all sleep together. Readers are to assume that sin like that would cause even Camelot's towers to tumble. I agreed. Society's rules are right, I thought; marriage vows are sacred and the only kind of respectable romantic love is for the opposite sex. But I intuited that Arthur's love for Lancelot was as right as that for Guinevere because both relationships were mutual and healthy. And so I was torn between what I considered to be two rights. This, I wrote in my high school journal, was a far more interesting conflict than the "man versus nature" or "man versus himself" of the English classroom. Arthur's undoing wasn't the result of a dualistic struggle between good and evil. It was his attempt to embody two incompatible goods: the love of his wife and the love of his best friend. The essence of his dilemma absorbed me.

Only with hindsight do I recognize how Arthur and Lancelot were, of all my reading, the only role models I could find who wrestled with what it means to love both men and women. I read their stories ceaselessly in an attempt to bring resolution to the conflict. Their ends were a dire warning. Lancelot went mad, romping naked in the woods. Arthur lost his kingdom to his illegitimate son and died an ignoble death. Guinevere wound up in a nunnery. They taught me that social mores ought to dictate behavior, and what we know in our hearts might better remain secret if we are to survive.

These days, when I remember my teenage self taking in these stories, I like to think about Arthur's final speech in Tennyson's version. "Pray for my soul," the dying king tells us. "More things are wrought of prayer than this world dreams of." I pray for his soul which is also the soul of those who have loved deeply and suffered by it. I pray that hurt from the past may be healed. I pray that my dreams may be far-reaching.

I crossed half the country to go to a maverick liberal arts college amid cornfields. There I was determined to begin anew. Among intellectual peers, I was sure that my brain would no longer be a roadblock to romance. All I needed to prove my sexual validity was a boyfriend, whom I searched for with a fervency I never permitted myself in high school. I snuggled next to Matthew in the concert hall as the orchestra played Ravel's *Bolero*, hoping he felt that amazing, repetitious crescendo as fully as I did. I endured lengthy one-way conversations about physics with John. I had a full-fledged crush on Cary Wentford, a senior who taught fencing in the PE department. At night I walked past the bright window of the dance studio where Cary practiced and watched him, dressed all in white, flashing his blunt-edged foil.

My relationship with God was as strained as these fleeting crushes. I was on my own and desperately homesick. The close comfort of my family, meals shared around the dinner table, nights of Scrabble with my parents and backwards backgammon with my sister, and the sacred intimacy that time taught me, was replaced with the drive to be coupled. I took in social and religious expectations for marriage without question. Fulfillment came with a mate, and so God must as well. It was a package deal, a theology of conformity thoroughly patriarchal and debilitating. The river was no longer out my window to remind me otherwise.

And so when Kyle placed a tentative kiss one night in the Japanese garden and suggested we see each other more seriously, I was swept away. Kyle was the son of not one but two Methodist pastors; in the context of our college's secular bent, he was impressively articulate about faith; he was subtly muscular and had sharp angles in his chin. His talk was straight as an arrow, usually with moralistic overtones, but he had a funny swing in his hips when he walked. His eyes sparkled when he spoke of his roommate. They also shone for me, and they were beautiful.

"I'm afraid I don't have the right kind of love for romance," I wrote in my journal at the beginning of our relationship, among many other nagging doubts that I soon suppressed. "I love it when he holds my waist and strains so hard to make me happy. But I cringe because something is missing." I was drawn, in a way, to Kyle's narrow cheekbones and well-shaped calves, and the confident way he spoke Christ's name during Bible study. I was drawn even more to the astonishing phenomenon that he thought me attractive. When we held hands walking across campus, suddenly I was validated. My body through his eyes was made beautiful in others' eyes. I was heterosexual after all, and whole by virtue of my attachment to a man. When we lay beside one another on the dormitory mattress, the muscles of our legs wrapped taut; when he pressed his fingers to the small of my back and pulled me firmly towards him; when I tasted his smooth teeth, his tongue and the supple wetness of his large lips, I was certain this was *God*, this pleasure, this connection so intense it had to be manifest in the joining of our bodies. The sweat on his shoulders afterward smelled sharp. That pungent smell kept me sleepless, restless, until I gave up Kyle's warm sheets and went out into the night back to my dorm. Kyle, I knew, lay awake fretting about the sin of bodily intimacy. I walked under the Minnesota stars with the space between my legs dull and aching. Half of me was elated and the other half chased after a fleeting suspicion that I could not pin down, that something essential was missing.

The Bible study Kyle and I belonged to was the group that taught me, to my astonishment, that faith didn't have to remain in the undercurrent of consciousness but could be articulated and debated. One evening in spring our discussion digressed from the scripture reading to the topic of lust. Josh Olson, a tall, Norwegian-blond Quaker soon to be born-again Christian, commented on how warm weather was a time of temptation for him. Studying moved outdoors and the clothes came off. He had to avert his eyes, he confessed, whenever he passed a woman. Safe in my new relationship with Kyle, I shared quite proudly that I enjoyed looking at everyone's bodies—I enjoyed watching my classmates' Minnesota winter skin turn brown, the bare-chested men leaping for frisbees and the women reading on the lawn in swimsuits. People are beautiful, I told Josh, and meant to be looked at. He was shocked. "I *don't*," I told him, "avert my eyes."

I took a life drawing class that term and grew accustomed to staring at models' private parts, so frustrated at not being able to accurately represent them on the page that I forgot to be embarrassed. The translation of fleshy curves into two dimensions was the biggest artistic challenge I ever faced. The female model, a floor-mate of mine, was skinny, and in my drawings her thighs flattened out like a paper doll's. The male model was easier because of the rounded muscles in his legs and forearms. But he took playful poses, hanging upside-down off a ladder or sitting backwards in a chair, despite our frustrated protests. I was in awe of how comfortable these models were in their bodies, and how still they could stay for twenty minute stretches. I loved their strange tan-lines and the quirks of their birthmarks. I thought I loved them with an artist's eye.

It was for drawing class as well that I first looked at my naked self in a full length mirror. I locked the dorm-room door with a fervent wish that my roommate wouldn't return early, pulled the curtains shut, and stripped. My page was large, three by two and a half; the charcoal stick turned the crook of my hand black. It was my collarbone that occupied me—the sharp cut of my shoulders done with hard lines, the hollow space at my throat softened with crosshatching. Drawing a self-portrait was a dangerous, exciting exercise.

My breasts hardened and I began to feel alive. *So this is what Kyle experiences when he touches me*, I thought. When I realized what was happening I dropped the charcoal and quickly rolled up the page. This was *wrong*, a voice in my head (Kyle's voice? God's voice?) said. With a swift dose of guilt I erased all self-pleasure. I learned not from my parents or from any overt teacher but through cultural osmosis that what pleasure was in my body belonged to a man. Arousing oneself is sinful; render unto Caesar what is Caesar's, to God what is God's, and a woman's body belongs to either but never to herself. When I unrolled the self-portrait for my teacher's critique, I looked at his paint splattered face and nodded. I refused to look at the page.

For three years Kyle and I dug ourselves deeper and deeper into disaster. I thought being coupled granted me sexual and social validity as a woman; he was convinced that my severe depression and insomnia had to do with female hormones and that the college psychologist would make things worse. I could describe the removed eye with which I came to watch our bodies interact—how my every bodily desire was initiated externally, how I observed him touching my face as though I were not behind it but hovering from a corner of the ceiling. I could tell how I rationalized away my premonitions by calling myself uptight or frigid. But this is a story many women know. I constructed a barrier between what might have sprung outward from my core had I loved the fullness and complexity of my impulses, and what was filtered inward, however pleasurable, through the skin. I played the role of lover well.

Those three years with Kyle are distorted by a curtain of tears. One Christmas break we visited his family in Iowa and endured the scrutiny potential life-partners are given by their parents. For the four-hour car ride home I cried incessantly. "I don't know what's wrong," I replied to Kyle's increasingly annoyed questions. "It has something to do with this image I have of the person I want to become." In secret, I conjured her up like a childhood imaginary friend. She wore her hair long, danced in sweeping circles, and made love fiercely. When Kyle asked what she was like, I panicked. Nothing would threaten her amazing beauty more than sharing her with Kyle. I kept her safe by shutting my mouth. She emerged only rarely, then, when my women friends and I drank coffee in the warm Saturday morning cafés, or when a line of poetry came spinning into my journal. She knew better than I what it is in others that excites me: an amalgam of a confident gait, reflective turn of chin, creative impulse and spiritual rootedness, with a strong voice that can cross the distance between two people. She knew Kyle did not have these. She was the source of my many tears because *she* was the missing piece—the wild, real Elizabeth with desires and dreams all her own.

Finally my relationship with Kyle dissolved into bitter discussions of gender equity and God. I was heavy into a course on liberation theology, and, at long last, in my junior year, had been exposed to feminist theory. My women friends and I spent hours drinking coffee and fuming at the patriarchy. I skipped church and Bible study. One hot spring day, sitting at the opposite end of the bed from Kyle, I finally blurted out, "You don't understand me the way my female friends do."

Kyle gave me a socially superior sneer. "You surround yourself with people and a God who agree with you," he accused. "You'll never grow up that way."

"Maybe God isn't exactly who you think He is," I shot back. This time I was determined not to buckle under his sharp, logical arguments. "Maybe there are healthier ways of relating than you want to admit."

"Maybe you should go off and be a lesbian," he retorted. "That seems like what you want." It was the most offensive comment he could think of, and I took it as low and cruel. But I wondered if it was an option. Nothing was for certain anymore.

My every construct crumbled when we broke up. I would not move into the safe, coupled realm of my parents' life immediately after college as I'd always expected; I would not graduate without first examining how I'd been duped into assuming that what others wanted was also what I wanted. And my conception of God was changing, from the smiling man I thought I loved into . . . unknowing, formlessness, the cause of this chaos. I had to get away. I bought airline tickets and made arrangements to spend fall term of my senior year biking then studying in Wales, away from Kyle, away from the small rural town surrounded by rolling farmland. Our parting at the Minneapolis airport was consistent with all other time we'd spent together: I cried and he pretended to be stoic, stuffing his hurt into hidden recesses that festered for years. At one point we had talked about marriage. I escaped just before that secret, dancing image of myself was suffocated.

Dormancy is the state of waiting. It is the duration of a restless season when verdancy pushes at the walls of a twig on a rose bush. It is the silent green pith of a branch that from the outside is indistinguishable from dead wood. We wake gradually from a period of sleeping; we wonder with growing awareness what neglect or infinite weariness put us under in the first place. The slow, thick sap which is our lifeblood begins to loosen in the veins; it begins to flow.

People are "meant to be green," Hildegard von Bingen was fond of saying. The life in us is meant to seep through the pores of our skin and reach in the sun's direction. As seemingly harmless as He was, the unchanging, omnipotent God of my upbringing allowed no room in His world for evolution or ambiguity. And so I thought there was no room for it in my world either. But all that time, deep in its core, my body knew otherwise. When I cut back the dead wood, I find this: All along I've been drawn to both men and women, aroused by how firmly a woman plants her feet on the ground or by the concentrated passion with which a man looks out a window. All along I've loved a multifaceted God. God creates by connecting disparate parts, by embracing paradox, by making of opposites (light and dark, death and life, male and female) an ever-changing whole.

I can feel it in my body.

Woman in a Wilderness

"Out? Why should I go out on a day like this?

"Well, if tha' doesn't go out tha'lt have to stay in, an' what has tha' got to do?"

The doorbell to the retreat center rings late one summer afternoon. I know who it is before I answer it, so on my way downstairs I grab a floppy, wide-brimmed hat and the key to the hermitage. Miriam has made reservations for a three-week retreat in our small, single-person dwelling out in the woods; she is changing jobs, moving from the emergency ward of a hospital to the directorship of a large, inner city missions project. We are the silent stopping place in between. For three weeks she will immerse herself in quiet—a long, deep breath in the middle of hectic years. Our responsibility is to nurture her alone-time with baskets of warm meals and prayer.

When I open the door, Miriam's youth surprises me. She's short and firmly built, with sandy hair that looks white in the sunlight. She sports hiking boots, jeans, and a Goretex jacket. I guess her age to be around thirty-five. From the moment I welcome her and take one of her bags, she is full of excited chatter. I calculate the years of her life as she talks:

taught for ten years in Catholic schools, worked in intensive care for twenty after doing some years abroad, was all set to do nursing in Africa when she was offered this directorship —an enormous responsibility but one she couldn't wait to get her hands on. She must be over fifty. We walk past the garden and into the woods. Her gait is sprightly; deer flies circle our heads and get caught in her hair, but she doesn't seem to mind.

I open the door and let her into the one-room hermitage. The building is surrounded by white pine and birch. Sun angles through the bay windows and is dappled across the wood floor and the back of the rocking chair. It's a simple room, but Miriam seems to think she's died and gone to heaven. She tests the quilted bed. She goes to the window and reads a small piece of calligraphy resting against the sill:

The Unforeseen Wilderness

And the world cannot be discovered by a journey of miles, no matter how long, but only by a spiritual journey, a journey of one inch, very arduous and humbling and joyful, by which we arrive at the ground at our feet and learn to be at home.

—Wendell Berry

I watch Miriam's back as she reads, suspecting that for her this inch is familiar territory. There is loneliness in the three weeks ahead, and doubt, and the weight of extended silence. She has packed lightly—one bag of clothes, one backpack of books and knitting. I tell her that I hope she will find solace and renewal in this place. She says, "I already have." For the next three weeks I see her daily in the kitchen when she picks up her meals. We don't say much. In this wilderness, she's traveling alone.

Miriam's disposition for retreat has its roots in the Catholic tradition—a built-in expectation that time apart is an essential element in spiritual formation. My tradition is the Protestant work ethic in which productivity is tied to the moral good, idleness to evil, and solitude to selfishness. I did not discover retreat by returning to the origin of my faith, although Jesus' routine of entering the wilderness helped justify it. I went on retreat in order to survive. Retreat rose up as part of a pattern of involvement and detachment, participation in the busy, beating heart of things and then separation to hear my own pulse. Retreat has been an act of defiance and, to an extent, desperation.

The first wilderness I ever crossed was the wilderness of a body I had not lived in since childhood. Literally, the journey took me miles up mountains and around the periphery of the Welsh countryside. But when I run my fingers over the borders on a map of Wales today, I know that everything abstract has its tangible counterpart. Frayed folds crisscross the country. The edges are water-stained with rain. A steady black line traces the remote roads, the B highways that bend up mountains instead of detouring around them; it figure-eights, backtracks and winds its way in a wide circle. The tiny gothic Ms marking monuments—the excavated cromlech, the stones said to be Arthur's throne—are circled, the hostels and campsites I inhabited so briefly are labeled, the visiting hours of castles are jotted in the margins. Occasionally there is a phonetic spelling beneath a Welsh town's name. I trace the black line of my retreat, remembering how the roads were paved and signs posted in English and a language full of mysterious consonants. When I look at the details of this map, it's clear that my journey was less than an inch. In the end, the place I learned to call home had walls of skin.

At the time, I assumed I was on a journey of miles. I had packed accordingly: bike panniers stuffed with a pump, helmet, sleeping bag and tent, a large spiral sketchbook, bags of books and papers for a semester at the University of North Wales at Bangor, a backpack of summer and winter clothes. I carried a miniature Revised Standard Bible that angered me every time I opened it because it was devoid of female pronouns. My address book had three pages newly changed: My parents had moved to Tokyo, my sister to Ghana, and Kyle (did I or didn't I want to write to him?) had moved to a rural town in southern Minnesota. I sat scrunched beside the rattling train window, knees to my chest because the bags took up all the leg room. The two-car train was empty. It rocked back and forth along the north coast of Wales, heading west from Chester. Watery sunlight flashed over empty seats. With its windows open, the train was a hull, loose and airy, which I hoped was transporting me away from the tangled mess of that romance.

I believed then what college students often believe—that traveling would transform me from the person I was into . . . someone more comfortable in the world? A woman in closer touch with what she calls sacred? I didn't own the words "spiritual journey" then, and that was good. Everything was solid as a result—a train, a small town at the end of the line, a mountain chain with narrow roads to climb on the back of a bike. I expected the natural elements to change me. The landscape would make me strong. The people's lilting Welsh accents would work on me like magic.

I chose Wales because it was the birthplace of the Arthurian legends and of my mother's father's ancestors. If my imagination had a home, it was on the coarse, Celtic countryside where stories are so much a part of the landscape that place names, long and tongue-twisting, are more narrative than nominal. My work was to pass through these towns. Their work was to transform me. The landscape I sought out took the shape of my shortcomings and questions. Wales, with its gorse-strewn hills and meandering stone walls, was my spiritual wilderness made solid.

The train careened between green-golden cliffs and the shimmering Irish Sea. I sat with my feet on my bags on the off-chance that the train would take on hordes of passengers before it reached Bangor. Only one woman boarded, at Conwy, carrying a worn riding saddle. She sat across from me with her head rested against the window frame. She made me feel foreign, not just in accent and appearance but in my body, with its cramped legs and frenzied hands folding and unfolding the map of Wales. I was ready to spring up at any moment because I was afraid I'd miss my stop. I felt most foreign because I was alone and didn't know who I was without family or friends to remind me. I kept looking over my shoulder.

Two nights earlier, on the other side of the Atlantic, my immediate family had gathered for dinner at a small Thai restaurant in Tarrytown. In preparation for a four-year assignment with IBM in Japan, my parents had pulled the curtains across our Hudson-view windows and locked shut the Pokahoe house. My father was thrilled by this major detour in his career path; my mother looked toward Asia with trep-idation. Marcy, now tall and letting her black hair grow long, had given up her effort to be happy at college. When she found herself retreating to the dorm-hall's broom closet to paint in peace, she realized she had to get out before it was too late. She was flying to Ghana to serve a year on a volunteer corps, working mostly with orphaned children. And I was off to Wales. Around a small corner table, the four of us raised goblets of milky Thai tea and toasted our re-spective adventures. The glasses clinked; we felt at once this unbearable love binding us and three corners of the world pulling us apart. The God I knew resided in the ring of four glasses. Was it possible to know God when I was spun out so far from this center? The empty pit in my stomach made me wonder.

At Penmaenmawr, a cement platform with a sign and a few cottages up the hillside, the woman rose across the aisle, flinging her saddle over her forearm. When she passed me, I breathed in leather and her tanned skin as though I could simply inhale everything I wasn't: confident, unashamed of the space I filled, easy in my limbs and sure of my destina-tion. From behind, her hair swung in a thick pendulum's arc. She leapt lightly to the platform.

The train slowed near Bangor. It was dusk and the sta-tion lamps were a dim yellow. I heaved on my pack and loaded my arms with bags. The train jerked to a stop; I stumbled forward. To unlatch the door, I had to reach out the open window and lift the external handle. The wooden frame swung outward. Between the train floor and the plat-form there was a gap of one inch, a dark chasm at the bottom of which the rails lurked. Unbalanced, tentative, I put forward a foot and then I had *arrived*, I was standing solidly in Wales.

My plan was to spend a few days in Bangor buying a bike and checking in at the university, then to hit the road for the month of September, not returning until classes started on October fourth. Where I got the inspiration to see the mountains from the back of a bike is a mystery; I was twenty and scarcely had a fit muscle in my body. The furthest I'd ever biked was thirty miles across the flat fields of central Minnesota. I bought my first biking shorts the week before I left the states, feeling self-conscious of how they molded my butt and thighs and assuring myself that I could wear them in Wales where no one knew me.

But when I woke the first morning in a cheap bed and breakfast, I could barely get myself out of bed, much less into lycra biking shorts. I tossed and tangled myself in the bed sheets, the soft mattress sagging beneath me. I had a head cold and a dread of beginning. From my window I could see Snowdonia, the highest mountain range in Wales. The mountains shifted and shouldered their weight as cloud shadows raced across their haunches. My route would take me directly into those monstrous thrusts of land. The sun was warm outside but the wind coming through my window had a bite to it, and I shivered under the covers. Whatever made me think I could take on this country alone? My gut churned. I suspected that my solitude over the coming month would not be the pleasing sort but would rather, as Thomas Merton wrote, frighten and empty me to the extent that I'd be exiled even from myself. This was not what I had intended.

The following morning I ventured down to the harbor, where the tide was out and sailboats lilted sideways in the silt, and back up to the town square bustling with shoppers. I hesitated by the clock, overwhelmed by ten hours of daylight to spend alone. Then I wandered in and out of bike shops, growing distressed at the price tags until I walked through the open door of a shop on High Street so small it housed maybe eight bicycles. Inside, the air hung with the pungent smell of grease. A wiry man eyed me warily and wiped his smeared hands on a rag. I explained my situation. I needed a durable, relatively inexpensive touring bike with low gears and as light a frame as possible. His eyebrows shot up. I'm spending a month touring, I said. He twisted the rag between his hands and stole nervous glances over his shoulder toward the back room, where I heard a bike wheel spinning. His obvious agitation made me uncomfortable. With a sudden motion he grabbed a pen and slip of paper and jotted down some numbers. "I have just the thing," he whispered. "But you'll have to call me at home."

Later that afternoon over the telephone he introduced himself as Gareth Davies, and apologized profusely for his behavior. "You see, it's my wife's bike," he explained, "and the manager at the shop . . . well, you understand." Within a half hour he pulled his white Fiat alongside the B&B, toting the bicycle in the trunk. It was sea-green, a Dawes twelve-speed with atrocious neon handlebars and chain wheels fitted for the mountains. I could lift it easily with one hand. "Don't you dare set out on your journey," he reprimanded me, "without first stopping for tea with me and Diana." Gareth and his bike had fallen from the heavens. Gripping my hand in a firm shake, he entrusted the bike to me, believing I'd have my travelers' checks cashed after the weekend and the money delivered before I headed out. He left me standing in the middle of the road, stunned.

For a few days I roamed the streets of Bangor waiting for the bank to open and regaining my health. Bangor is squeezed in a cove where the Irish Sea must have once washed up. When the tide is low, the harbor reeks with a thick fishy muck, and when it's high the painted boats bounce on the waves, their rigging ringing against the masts. At the north end of town, past the university, Bangor borders the Menai Strait. During certain seasons you can stand on the bridge between Bangor and Anglesey, the island of the druids, and watch the jellyfish tumble and roll in the current. There is an old Roman camp overlooking the strait where it is said the Normans rallied their forces before taking Anglesey. They lined up along the coast while on the opposite shore, a quarter mile across, the druids beat drums and shouted prayers. The druidic women tore off their clothes and danced wildly, naked, screaming sorcery at the Normans. Anglesey was the last corner of Wales to be conquered by the Christians.

I checked in at the university and stowed my belongings in the basement of a women's dormitory. At the top of the hill stood the library, with Gothic, grey-stone walls and towering stained glass windows. I entered with awe: The books in this place were where my childhood fantasies had their historic origins. On the dusty shelves I found leather volumes of the *Mabinogion*, Nennius' *Annals Cambrae*, Geoffrey of Monmouth's tomes, the travels of Gerald of Wales and the magical *Red Book of Hergest*—all half fact, half legend, all assuming the distinction was irrelevant. Here were the first ninth-century hints of King Arthur slipped between lines of a ballad. Here pagan goddesses acquired thin Christian masks and romped on horseback across pages of text. I fingered the spines of these ancient books, eager for my studies to begin.

Back out in the cold sunshine, I found all of Bangor's compact streets nestled at my feet. I descended, bought a warm meat pasty at the bakery, and decided to get a closer look at Snowdonia. To go anywhere in Wales I'd have to bike into those mountains. At the south end of High Street I locked my bike to a lamp post and found a path climbing to the rise above the bay. At the top I'd see eight flat miles of grazing land and then the base of the mountain range. I wanted to witness the challenge ahead of me. I wanted to measure myself against the landscape. The hiking path wound through scraggly brush and thick-leafed foliage. The air had the luminescence of September light in the early evening that makes one feel distant from the earth. Under my feet the gravel was loose and dry. Shingled roofs appeared below me through the trees. The rhythm of climbing calmed me.

I rounded a bend halfway up and stopped short. There was a woman lying face down in the path. She had on tan slacks and a plaid polyester blouse. Her nose was in the sand. Above her head the pale flab of her forearm was stretched awkwardly. At the small of her back, along her waist, her shirt had pulled from her pants to expose a raw inch of skin. All at once I felt sick. I knelt down at her feet and pushed her roughly, croaking, "Are you okay?" She was unresponsive, a sack of flour. *"Are you okay?"* Dust from the path was on her cheek. I was shaking too hard to tell if she was breathing.

Time stopped. I was alone in a foreign country, a solitary woman at the northern edge of Wales. I had climbed the hill to see the landscape I'd be crossing over the next month and found instead this woman, prostrate and vulnerable, ground into the dirt. I couldn't tell if she was in despair or drunk or if she had fainted or if she'd been assaulted or . . . .

And then I could no longer think. My insides screamed. All I knew was impulse, a blind, tripping impulse that sent me cascading down the path, stumbling and sliding past the blur of bushes until I came to the street. I hit the pavement, fumbled with the bike lock, and careened, half crazy, among the few shoppers left in town, down the rows of houses to the bed and breakfast where I let myself in and raced up the stairs to my room. I collapsed face first on the bed. With a sharp intake of breath I flung myself over to face the ceiling—otherwise I'd be in *her* position. The air in my lungs was short and hacked. The words I had not spoken to any stranger or police officer choked me. I could not name aloud or even in my head what I had seen. Most horrifying was my own silence. It was seven o'clock in the evening, still daylight. In my mind's eye I watched the sky turn dark above that woman's back. I saw the stars come out, the wind pick up, and the trees bend over her destitution.

I ached for that woman. She had no one to care for her in her crisis, no stranger even to offer a hand. What abject destitution she must know! At the same time, it seemed that her vulnerability lived inside me. I knew the slight twist of her ankle and how sand and stones pushed into her facial tissue. I knew these details from photographs in the daily newspaper, women abducted or abused or murdered, women I had thought didn't live carefully or knew the wrong people but who I now saw were just women alone in the world. Every woman faces these possibilities when she turns off the main road and heads up a side path. I knew her tussled hair and spread fingers as though from a fairy tale told in my childhood to help me know fear. Or I knew them more intimately even than that. Suddenly my journey was not a simple matter of passing over a landscape. A part of me had appeared in my path. Fear had manifest itself in flesh.

My reflexes were to flee. I did not alert professional help. I did not put a finger to her thick white throat to find a pulse. I did not roll her over so she could breathe. Touching her in that way would have meant touching my fear. Asking for help would have meant acknowledging my weakness. So I turned my back on her, on myself, just as Jesus taught us not to in the parable of the Good Samaritan. Had I helped her, there'd be more to trust in the world. But now a woman was out there, uncared-for, her body yearning to be healed. She wailed inside of me all night long. I did not sleep.

The next morning I lay in bed, paralyzed. If I chose to rise, to pack my panniers and mount the bicycle that had appeared *machina ex Deo*, then I was also choosing the possibility that at any moment in the next month my bike might tip on some abandoned road, I might be raped or robbed or car-wrecked, and the people who stumbled upon me might leave me there to die just as I had abandoned the woman. This was the world I had helped create. I knew I had to travel into my fear. I crawled out of bed. It took me hours to fold clothes, faltering over every sock and tee-shirt. On the street I hooked the panniers to the rear wheel, tied down the tent and sleeping bag, and heaved my sleepless limbs over the crossbar.

The roads were crowded with Monday morning traffic rushing toward me from the wrong side. My bike was overloaded, made heavier with guilt. I wobbled dangerously along the edge of the pavement. At the Davies' cottage, Gareth and Diana welcomed me with tea and scones. Gareth pranced around my bike and lent me a light jacket to take instead of my wool sweater. Their care did little to calm me. Another woman's tongue was caught in my throat, preventing me from voicing my worries. Fatherly and concerned, Gareth walked me to the road and waved.

I pedaled out of the coastal towns, away from clusters of cottages and trees and up to the pastures at the foot of the mountains. Climbing, I grew overheated and short of breath. A car passed and my front wheel flipped into the gravel shoulder; I over-compensated, swinging my bike into the center of the road. Halfway up, exhausted, I collapsed in a grassy culvert. My lungs were stinging. I had biked five miles. I wished Gareth would happen to drive past and rescue me.

Later that day I scrawled in my journal:

September 1

"Then Jesus was led up by the Spirit into the wilderness to be tempted by the devil," Matthew wrote in the fourth chapter. Wilderness meant forty days of starvation, followed by the three temptations. What fascinates me about this story is not the devil hissing into the ear of Christ and not that power which we nonetheless believe Jesus possesses, to turn stone into bread, to leap off towers into the arms of angels, to call his own the land stretching across all the nations. What draws me is that mysterious Spirit which led Jesus into that misery in the first place.

What happened to the loving parent-God? I don't understand a Spirit who deliberately leads us into disaster, who forsakes us in the name of refining the flawed core of our souls. "Lead us not into temptation," I was taught to chant on Sunday mornings; keep that devil at bay, and by all means don't hand me over intentionally.

In the first quaint village I passed through, a pack of teenagers heckled me from the street corner. I was exposed to the wind on the open road, to speeding lorries and glass shards on the pavement. All day I was out of breath. The pasture land I rode through was green, but it felt strangely barren. Where was God? Where was God for that woman? Where was God that I'd come across her, and that I didn't have courage to help? I clung to remnants of that omnipotent, all-forgiving Father because I thought they gave me hope. His plan was bigger than mine. His role was Comforter.

But then Jesus came through it all right. In a selfish, sadistic way, it's satisfying to know that he, too, experienced a dry tongue and the desire to fall into God's arms. Not that another's suffering is much comfort in the middle of my own. But afterward, when I look back over this journey, perhaps it will resonate with a little more meaning. Perhaps I will find that wilderness is natural territory in my broader landscape.

Beneath my optimism was nagging doubt. If there was meaning in a single woman's destitution, it was not something I could bear. That day I pedaled ten miles, most of them steep. Llanberis Pass cut into Snowdonia at an angle, turning away from the afternoon sun. While I was straining to feel God's presence, I rode along the valley past steep slopes mined for coal. Slag heaps and dark mine entrances covered the hillsides. At their bases they touched the surface of lakes—Llyn Padarn, Llyn Peris, falling into early dusk.

I stopped in the town of Llanberis. The castle there once corked up the pass to prevent Norman access to Gwynedd, Wales' northern region; I wandered between the rubble of its walls. Nothing of its former strength was left except one round tower. But its placement was good, blocking the hollow between two impassable mountains. Thin strips of lake reflected on either side. Above a wide cut of sky spread the length of the valley, sculpted on either edge by sharp peaks. The daylight seemed interminable to me—in fact, the entire month ahead was a wasteland of time reaching as far as the walls of these mountains. I lay on my back, a rough slab of stone cutting into my spine, and watched the blue sky darken with evening. What would I possibly do with myself in all this time, in this immense landscape?

And yet I sensed that my placement was right. Even if all else was crumbling, I was strategically positioned. The mountains on either side would challenge and protect me. They strained skyward, green and black and magnificent. I longed to be as strong as they were, to be a woman worthy of a loving God. I longed to be unafraid to feel for another's pulse. I longed to know my own pulse, beating with all this fierce beauty.

Ornery and aching, I remounted my bike and rode up the high end of town to the hostel, a clapboard farmhouse with a sweeping view of the pass. I sat on the porch watching shadows creep up the opposite slope, the mountains' tips turning scarlet, until it was too chilly to be outdoors. Inside, the common room was bare. A crooked billiards table took up the center space and straight-backed chairs lined the walls. I tried to get comfortable in the corner, curled up with my journal and pen. My handwriting was terse and looping, full of religious discomfort and formulaic language. I kept shifting in the hard seat.

Eventually the room's empty walls drove me up to the women's dormitory, an angular room with five sets of metal bunk beds. I knelt at my pack to dig for a better pen when I noticed two other women in the room, sitting on the top bunk by the window. They faced one another the way my sister and I used to sit on our worn living room sofa—legs spread apart and bare feet touching. When we were in a good mood Marcy and I would talk that way, and then we'd fall back, moving our feet together through the air as though pedaling a common bicycle. These women leaned slightly toward one another, speaking Welsh in an undercurrent of breath. To my foreign ears the airy vowels and earthbound gutterals made their talk intimate. Or was it how unafraid they were to look into each other's eyes while speaking? Evening sun crossed the mattress and their outstretched legs—it lit the hands they clasped between one another until that corner of the room burned with light. Strands of amber and gold shone in their loose hair. I knelt by the doorway, unnoticed. They shifted to give one another back-rubs, one kneeling into the thin mattress while the other turned her head slightly to the side on the pillow. Together this way, the women were so stunning I had to leave the room.

Their love left me tongue-tied. Standing in the hall, my back turned to their radiance, I felt the chasm between what

I assumed I had wanted in my relationship with Kyle (his fingers on my face convincing me I was loved, making me whole) and what I ached for, connection sprung not from need but from genuine delight. The love between Kyle and me had been obligatory, routine, pattered by well-worn expectations. Someone outside of us—our parents? our culture?—had written a story which we'd then lived out as though it was our own. It was empty of passion and genuine individuality. It was not unlike my love for God. Touching Kyle, my body was customary and, obvious to everyone, a heterosexual woman's body. Apart from him I was no longer sure.

Two women awash in sunlight and in whispered words started still wheels turning within me. I loved their love. I loved the ease and unabashed presence they brought to one another. It was possible that what one saw in the other's eyes I might see in myself, or in someone else. It was possible that the girl who pedaled her sister's feet could bring herself, now a woman, fully and with wild, cycling abandon into relationship—with a friend, with a lover, with God. Every day of the following month, and long afterward, the murmur of the women's Welsh surrounded me like the swish of spokes through the air. The sun on their hair and joined hands had blessed them. It blessed my memory when I thought of them. They came with me like angels, pulling me across difficult times and into the light.

September 2

How can I sing the Lord's song in a foreign land if that land is myself? Where can I learn to sing so that my voice is confident, my words distinct bits of praise and my song in the shape of who I am? The psalmists did it; why shouldn't I? I pray for the courage to try, but it's frightening and a barrier has prevented me that I've never been able to overcome except in my imagination. I pray that the barrier could break down and you and I, God, could sit on the top bunk together like sisters or lovers in an imaginary world, your world made right.

I came down from Snowdonia carrying this image of God like a snapshot in my shirt pocket. The barrier between who I was and who I longed to be, I believed, resided somewhere on the Welsh countryside, and now I was rolling down its slopes collecting speed, preparing to break through it. I hunched over the handlebars holding so tightly my hands cramped. Every muscle—in my shoulders, down my back, where my butt bounced on the seat—was strained from the previous day. The weight of my luggage gave me speed I couldn't control. I looked mostly at the pavement.

When the land leveled and I turned westward out the Llyn Peninsula, Wales' skinny left arm, the riding grew smooth. The rural roads on that extension of land twisted drunkenly between blackberry hedges until suddenly the water spanned out and the horizon widened. The weather was fine. Sheep grazed beside the beaches, and my spirits rose. I swerved down the center of the road avoiding the thorny clippings from a recent pruning. For hours I encountered no cars. The land was a rich, rolling green, and the sea was as blue as the sky.

By early evening, though, the sky turned grey, and I pulled my bike into a campground. I found a dry spot beside a stone wall in a grassy clearing by the sea and pitched my tent. The wind tore the nylon flaps away from my cold hands. The aluminum poles trembled.

When I rose from pitching the tent, I stood taller than any object along the coast. The beach was all stones. Sticky succulent weeds lay about like scarves tossed from the sea's angry shoulders. The tide had created channels among the stones, and I followed their paths as they curved and backtracked on their route to the mother-water. The waves tossed fist-sized rocks as though they were sand. A roar louder than any the Hudson ever makes took up all my thinking space. With the company of my own voice erased, I felt suddenly and completely alone. No one in the entire world—not my family, not a single stranger—knew where I was. The sea was deafening. Storm clouds heaved up to the mainland. I stumbled my way back to the tent.

I fell asleep easily enough, but then woke bolt upright in the middle of the night. The incoming waves sounded monstrous. Something icy and wet was near me; I reached out of the sleeping bag and panicked—the tent walls were half collapsed and soaked—with what? Ocean spray? Had I misjudged the tide and staked the tent too close? But then I heard a breaker that was too sharp to be water, a crack like the world had broken its neck, and I knew the sky was thundering and rain flooding sideways off the sea. I tried to hear a rhythm to the waves and to convince myself it was comforting. But it was a bombardment, a maniac's lullaby.

Where was God now? The words of the Welsh poet Idris Davies rose from my shivering hysteria: "Even God is uneasy, / say the moist bells of Swansea." Only I mis-remembered them and heard instead "Even God isn't easy." No, God was not going to bend nature's path or steer me clear of loneliness; no, God would not stop this sinking at midnight into the moist sod of depression. I was cold, a wet woman alone beside the raging Irish Sea, and God would do nothing to comfort me. I curled up into a fetal tuck.

In the morning I regretted waking. The storm had calmed itself down to a grey mood, and cold rain curtained off the sea. I was lying in a puddle between collapsed tent walls. The pasty I had bought for breakfast looked cold and greasy through the fog of its plastic wrapper. I gave myself over to inertia. I could choose a sluggish, damp death or a wet ride across the peninsula to a bed and breakfast. Only after serious consideration did I struggle out into the mist.

I rode south with a rain hood strapped beneath my helmet and found a bed and breakfast in Pwllweli. The bed sagged but was warm. As I strung wet clothes across the open window, I thought of Dylan Thomas writing poems in little rented rooms all over Wales. Certainly he also squandered money for a dry room in order to write words he later left crumpled in a dust bin. I wrapped myself in blankets and wrote in my journal. After dark the sounds of a child practicing piano stumbled through the stone alleyways. I fell asleep to *Für Elise*.

September 3

There are voices in the rain, voices that cry out and chill my bones. I hear them especially when I am alone, because then they drip down into my ear and ring until I shiver. These voices call me foolish and small, and challenge my ambitions. Climbing the hill this morning, face into the wind, all the dripping mist of the mountains said to me, "Why?" and laughed with a hiss. The voices soaked my bags and shoes and sweat pants; they wet my face until I couldn't tell what was tears, what was rain or what was my dripping nose. They are convincing, and I wonder if I really can make it alone, or want to. The rain laughs one final "Ha!" as I check into this B&B, then turns silent and gives way to the birds. Why, after all?

The next morning dazzled, the piercing blue iris of a divine eye. I left Pwllweli with the ocean fringing the banks at my left and the shag-green of sheep fields at my right. I cheered as pheasants plucked seeds from cracks in the pavement and then raced recklessly ahead of my bike. When I stopped to pick from the untrimmed blackberry brambles lining the roads, their fruit stained my palms with wine. After the previous day's rain, each moment under the warm sun felt like a gift. Invigorated, I followed the coast out to the peninsula's tip.

In the town of Aberdaron I ate a ploughman's lunch of bread and cheese and then backtracked, this time along the Llyn's north shore and once again across its girth. I walked the clean-cut edges of Criccieth castle, bought groceries, and debated: Should I stay put in the luxury of a bed and breakfast or push onward to the hostel in Ffestiniog? On the map the distance measured an inch; I figured one more hour of riding. It was early evening. Already I had gone fifty miles that day, and was curious to test my body's endurance. I loaded up my packs and turned inland.

Between the coastal towns of Portmadog and Penrhyn-deudraeth the land was so flat a bridge had been built where the tide spilled over. Suddenly the road swung upward. I began to feel the seven hours I'd spent on the bike's hard seat pulling inside my muscles. Lorries belched exhaust in my face as they strained uphill. The few steep feet of gravely blacktop before my front wheel became my scenery and I didn't stop to take pictures. The name of my destination—Ffestiniog—festered in my brain until its hashed consonants took the blame for every inch of painful gradient in the road that led there. My lungs ached, my eyes stung with dust, my forearms twitched and cramped, and all the while the wind fought against me.

Just as the air turned to dusk, I careened down the dirt drive to the youth hostel. It was closed—closed by the whim of the warden because it was Thursday. Sitting on the steps, I tried to spread cream cheese on crackers for dinner, but I'd lost my fine motor skills with hours of too much strain and no nourishment. I had broken my body's boundaries with these last three hours of riding, and was shaking so hard I couldn't cry. Afraid to remount my bike, I wheeled it up the drive and to a bed and breakfast across the street, for which I was grateful only later, after a round matron served me a cheese sandwich cut in triangles and I could breathe again. Fully clothed, shivering under a down comforter on the bed, I didn't sleep. Ffestiniog was quiet, a mountain town. But there was a ringing in my ears.

The following day I heaved my protesting limbs over the bike frame and began the descent out of the mountains. My feet rested in their toe clips; I let gravity do the work. For a full half hour I coasted downward without the least effort. *From now on*, I promised my body, *I will listen to you. I will respect your needs and desires.* Saying this surprised me. It had never before occurred to me to listen to my body. That day, all it wanted was an effortless flight downhill and to see the landscape it had missed during the climb up. I watched mist rise from crevices of mountainside and stone walls run heedlessly along steep slopes. After a struggle the sun broke through and soaked the air with humidity. The hills were a sheer green. It was an exacting beauty, a landscape without compromise. I was grateful that I had chosen to ache out my limitations on this beauty. *I want to be as strong as these hills*, I told God. *I want to weather as these hills weather, wind-torn and storm-worn and flooded with sun.*

I returned again to the coast, heading south along the Harlech cliffs where, in the Welsh legend, Bendigeifran's soldiers heard "a certain song, and of all the songs they had ever heard each one was unlovely compared with that." It was the song of birds who were messengers of Rhiannon, the Celtic goddess. "And far must they look to see them out over the deep, yet was it as clear to them as if they were close by them." In bits and snatches, I began to hear the song as well. I heard it because I was alone and had slowed down. I could be lured into listening.

I took my time meandering south. In the beach town of Borth I spent a cold Sunday morning on a bench outside a country church. Women in cotton skirts and men in black trousers climbed the steps while I felt the pull of an obligation. After all, I *was* looking for God. But I couldn't work up the energy to socialize with strangers. I wasn't dressed right. I didn't want to spend a sun-swept day indoors. I wasn't up to sitting on stiff pews, tracing the worn patterns of liturgy in the air. Instead, I walked to the beach. I sat in the sand and drew patterns there. Instinct said I knew the God of church too well. That morning I wanted to worship the God of the open road.

Further down the road I found a more fitting sanctuary. Perched above the water was a cemetery whose rusted gate had been left open. I leaned my bike against the first Celtic cross. The gravestones had been laid without regard for the way the land sloped down to Cardigan Bay, so they were pulled by gravity or erosion into reverent positions, stone bowing to water. Most of the deceased had been buried once with rocky soil and then again with rampant ivy. The further I walked, the denser the ivy became, concealing the lives and deaths of entire families. I didn't notice the stone ruins of a church until I was on top of it. I bushwhacked my way to a window. Gorse and ivy filled the worship space; the walls were open to a salty blue sky. Everything about the place was death in partnership with untamed life. Had I a gallon bucket I could have climbed through and filled it with blackberries. Here was a place I could praise my maker.

I found a place to sit. The bend of land looked north and west. There, in the distance, was the Llyn Peninsula pointing its thick finger southwestward into the Irish Sea. It was on that landscape that loneliness had shaken me like thunder and I had curled into a ball for protection. The soggy campsite seemed minute now, on the other side of the horizon's edge. I suspected God's comfort of being more subtle or basic than the dramatic cessation of wind and lightening I had longed for that night. God was broad as the land was broad and could be seen with perspective rarely. It occurred to me with amazement that I had traveled the peninsula from the hazy tip to its marshy underarm. My body had taken me that distance. I was seeing the earth's enormity for the first time, my mind's eye opening to the land's presence as I rolled over it. Something in me shifted. I could propel myself from there to here; I could cover ground. And ground could cover me. Even when I was all alone, there was this fundamental relationship with the world. I reached down and rubbed a dark leaf of ivy between my fingers. Its smell was lively, green and pungent.

Finally I turned my back on the water and its fishing villages and headed eastward, upward, into the Cambrian Mountains. The road I chose resigned itself to the contour of the landscape; it did nothing to interrupt the view or make the gradient easier. As I climbed, the grazed hills began to yellow with an early autumn. Traces of stone walls thinned and sheep grew bold, darting in front of me with assertive, woolly tails. Eventually there were no walls at all. The wind swept over the tops of these balding inclines without interruption, except for me, perched on my bicycle. The high, silent country of Wales rolled out gold at my feet.

Hours passed on the empty land. It was so quiet that the prattle of my thoughts grew raucous. How were my parents handling culture shock in Tokyo? Was Marcy lonely in the orphanage in Ghana, where children stroked the light hairs on her arms? Kyle, I knew, was in the Midwest reeling from our breakup. Had he written? Strangely enough, I thought about the small Methodist congregation I had grown up in, whose elderly members brought baked beans to potlucks and included me in their devotions. The prayers of these people were like the black lines and blue dotted channel crossings that connected points on the world map. They supported and guided me even from a distance. When I cried on the road, remembering the woman I had neglected to help, the wind smeared my tears sideways. It had been two weeks since anyone had touched me.

I tried to talk with God. I tried to focus on a piece of wisdom, like the verse from Romans about how suffering builds character and hope. But my concentration scattered cross-winds. "Place is never so powerful as when it is suffered in silence," Eavan Boland writes. Loneliness on its recurring cycle took up space. It took the distance of every uphill push, it sat on bare rock at the hill's head, it plunged down the trickle of road into the valley. The sky up in those mountains was a thin blue. Eventually my thoughts grew quiet. The only thing left filling the vastness of a day was my body's movement—the short spin of pedals, the bend and stretch of my back.

The hostels in those remote hills were peopled sparely by wiry old men traveling on three-speed bikes who found it imperative to instruct me on the proper manner to patch a tire. There were also a few German fellows vacationing after their tour of duty; one man picked light brown mushrooms (chanterell and penny bun) and gave me a ladle of stew in exchange for some rice. For a week I did not speak with another woman. For days I did not speak with anyone except to lay down a five-pound fee at the hostel register. Slowly I allowed being alone to grow on me like burying ivy.

At a forlorn hostel whose front door was so low I had to stoop to enter, I spent two days listening to my tired body. I had originally intended to push all the way down into Cornwall to see Tintagel, the mythological birthplace of King Arthur, until I realized I was motivated more by ego (the pride I'd take in telling others how far I'd gone) than by desire. After Ffestiniog, I owed my ego nothing. Instead I let the warm afternoons slow me down. I hiked up a stream that cut a dark iron swath through the pastures. Walking felt easy, unburdened. At a grassy bend in the stream, I lay down and slept soundly in the sun. In the evening I sat on a bench in the kitchen and let my bare feet soak up the cold from the floor's large slate slabs. As soon as the light dimmed, a cat slinked in along the far wall and curled up next to the empty fireplace. The windows were wide open. I spread out my map, flattened the grid of folds, and traced my route up an unlabeled road to this unnamed place. The sprightly old warden in knickers called it "Dolgach," so I penned the name in and wrote it again at the top of a blank journal page.

Dolgach, September 15

Oh God, I call on you often in my heart, not out of devotion or piety but out of a lack of anyone else to talk to. I say your name and then my thoughts scatter—to the wall-less pastures, to the meal I will make tonight, to the people who have inhabited my world and for whom I'm grateful. But I can't focus on you, faceless, nameless I Am. Abstraction defies me when my back aches from bending and this hill I am climbing seems eternal. Is it heresy, then, to worship the firmness of the road I am on? Or the rare tree I find in these Black Mountains? Or the wind itself? Right now, these are all I know for company and really they are who I speak to. Wales has made me pagan, God, or has fractured you into a myriad of tangible parts.

The warden came in with a pail of coal and tsked at finding me bent over paper in the early twilight. He scurried off to retrieve "just the thing"—a stub of red wax sticking crookedly out of a monstrous, well-dented candlestick "which," he boasted, "I stole from the Vatican." With shaking, gnarly hands and a match he lit it for me. Then, using breath from the hand bellows and a shovel of coal, he sparked the flames the cat knew lay buried in the fireplace ashes. Building fires made him tired, he told me, and for that there was only one remedy. He plunked himself down at a century-old pump organ and began working the pedals with a vigor I supposed came from his second wind. It was "Men of Harlech," wheezed from pipes and bounding off the room's stone walls. He showed me how to light the gas lamps so I could light my own in the women's dormitory before bed. "You must strike the match; whistle, like this"—a raspy, musical blowing—"and turn the little knob. See? It works!" The room came alive with our shadows, ironed flat on the floor and cutting a sharp corner upward at the wall. Whistling was the trick.

I spent those nights in a dead sleep. Cold air came through the open window. When I woke to the bleating of sheep, I lay flat, in the exact position I'd fallen asleep. Exhaustion privileged this escape. Night was effortless and unmemorable.

God, as Annie Dillard writes, was splintered. What I couldn't grasp as an abstraction I came to worship in small pieces of matter: the flick of a sheep's tail, the moment before a hill's crest when suddenly the climb eases, the lone neolithic stones erect in some farmer's field. It wasn't paganism, really, but panentheism—the world as immanation, Dillard explains: "God in the thing, and eternally present here, if nowhere else." Even when the wind blew so hard I had to pedal downhill, and uphill leaned flat across my handlebars as though they were a horse's back; even remembering the storm on the Llyn Peninsula, I suspected God of being in the wind. God wasn't all comfort, good fortune and easy company. There was no place and no created thing where God wasn't.

I hoisted this suspicion onto the back of my bike. Now I was saddle-worn. The eighty-mile-day of a week ago, culminating at Ffestiniog, had put the worst not behind me but inside of me, memorized in the strained tan of my calves. My water bottles were full and warm; I casually snacked on peanuts tucked into the handlebar bag. My panniers, trailing underwear and socks washed in a sink that morning, held everything I needed. I was self-sufficient and mobile. The sea-green bike no longer begrudged me of forward movement; it held me high above the grill of the road and sometimes let me fly. The bike had fine-tuned my limbs and tempered my ambition. Seated on my bicycle, I found the center of my body's gravity, and it was in motion.

September 19

This is a wild place, and it's all being pumped into my bloodstream. Wales is changing my body, the hills are becoming my muscles and the wind my breath. When I come away from Wales I'll be shaped by rain and blackberries and mornings when sunshine washes me awake. I'm surprised to find happiness even when I'm alone. Each day is a miracle of accomplishment. When I sleep I know I've traveled so far, just me and God, and I've fed myself and filled my head with thoughts, however worthy or worthless.

The pattern of a journey sinks into our bodies; change becomes our life-breath and destinations become irrelevant. In Wales my forearms grew thick from holding my torso over the bike frame, but it was the substance of transformation that fleshed out those muscles and filled my lungs. Before I could recognize a flash of God in my body, I recognized change.

At the Brecon hostel, which was filled with rambunctious Girl Guides, I teased the eleven-year-olds as we competed for slices of garlic bread at the dinner table and taught them to sing "Country Roads" beside the fireplace. At White Castle I relished having an entire Norman fortress to myself for an afternoon. I sketched an arrow window and the flowering purple weeds growing between stones. Something in me had eased; I had grown confident in my own company. In Monmouth I stayed in an old parish rectory with arched windows and long echoing halls still connected to the church, where the congregation was sharing a Harvest Festival meal. They left a loaf of bread in the kitchen for us travelers. When a swaggering Scotsman slipped the loaf into his bag, I shouted across the room, "Hey! That was meant for everyone!" He pretended to be surprised. My bold shout made the young man eating across the table from me look up. With a lock of dark hair hanging in his eyes he said, "You must be biking." "How can you tell?" I asked. He pointed the round end of his fork to the back of my hands. Fingertips to knuckles were tanned, and where my biking gloves velcroed across the back of my wrist was a swath of white skin. They were not the hands I'd begun with. After dinner I went into the chapel, which was decked with gourds, corn husks and autumn dried flowers. Facing the altar I made fists then splayed my brown fingers wide. *For whatever you're making of me*, I prayed to God, *I thank you.*

Wales redrew my internal map. I had wanted to move from here to there, from a point of prostrate vulnerability to one of confidence and independence. I had wanted to *arrive*. But movement over the landscape—from Chepstow up the Wye and Golden Valleys, out toward Shrewsbury then back into Wales and the mountains—movement and the changes it wrought became the goals, the ends of the journey. Wales drew into my map a wilderness and a confluence of many streams. Blue bloodlines tied one remote town to another all the way around the world. Certain landmarks grew familiar. They marked both the distance from home and home itself, which I discovered I carried in my gut like the center-weight balanced on my bike. When I came to the border between England and Wales, it seemed simultaneously arbitrary and significant. The flatlands of Shropshire ended at the wall of Wales, where steep mountains forced me to slow down again. Wales was a woman denied her political identity, and yet her boundaries were as clear as the gradient in the road and the lilting tongue spoken on small town streets. Wales redrew my map, labeled the new country "woman," and humbled me with the reminder of my interdependence.

The Llangollen Dee cut a pass into the Berwyn Mountains; I followed the narrow, rushing water as it bent and twisted between houses and yellowed slopes. Corwen, Llandrillo, Rhos-y-gwaliau, homes clustered on hillsides declaring themselves villages, weeds growing from cracks in the pavement and well-tended, enclosed gardens now going to seed. On the north bank of the Alwen Dee my front tire hit a thorn and deflated over the next fifteen yards: my first puncture. I patched it (thanks to my own skill and not the advice of the men in the Black Mountains) while sun and rain alternated on my back. In Bala I stopped at a vegetable shop where a friendly Welshman who spoke no English sold me potatoes, leeks and a cochet. Sun skimmed over the surface of Llyn Tegid. The hostel was a stone manor house with clotheslines strung across the courtyard. I slept beside the leaded panes of an open window. In the morning, fog gathered in the enclosed front garden and draped the apple tree. I went out and picked wet-skinned apples, boiling them into sauce for breakfast over a single-burner stove.

When I pedaled out of the valley my tires cut through a covering of mist that hid the pavement. The lake was erased entirely. Lurking shadows along the street became the row houses of Bala, unfolding from their shrouds. I climbed in altitude until I emerged above the clouds, and then stopped to watch the veil lift itself above the cut fields, retreating fence posts, stone homes and, gradually, the sky all blue and penetrating. Fog burned from the water's surface until the lake mirrored the sky. The higher the road took me, the smaller it grew until at one point I had to open and close cattle gates in order to continue. Sheep stared at me dumbly then scampered from my path. By noontime I had crossed a worn range of mountains unnamed on my map. The late September sun was no longer warm. But it was vainglorious.

I stopped to drink in the moment. At my feet my route wound down, dipping momentarily behind cropped knolls and emerging below where it converged with the main road. Overgrown hedgerows sectioned off the fields beneath me. The rise of Gylchedd at my back and the steeper Cambrian peaks to the northwest were splashed with cloud shadows. In my lungs the air was clear; in my mouth I tasted autumn.

I dismounted and stood on the hard-packed road. Often in Celtic myths and ballads, a miracle will rescue a woman from some danger (the shame of an unwarranted inspection of her virginity, for example, or the ravaging anger of an unwanted suitor) by transforming her: She grows roots and sends out branches, and her true love becomes a wind sighing among her leaves. I felt suddenly planted, as though the earth were pulling my limbs toward her soiled core. My body sprang from the mountain rock. I stretched my fingers wide, my hands open and arms out-flung. With inside eyes I saw my taut muscles, tanned skin, the balance between one leg and the other and one arm and the other, the pull of ribs and full lungs, my strong shoulders and firm back, tussled hair and the cool sweat of my thighs. My breasts were firm. The wind made my eyes water. Everything in me shivered. Every sheep and scraggly stump of grass on the hillside I saw with liquid clarity. I saw roiling white clouds and their shadows, malformed and elapsing over the landscape, as a form of praise, and I saw the rarely traveled road beside me as full of praise. The creator was reckless and embracing. The creator's image included all this and it included me, the prickling chill on my skin, the impulse that pulled from my core a wild, erotic connection to the land. With a deep breath I knew for the first time where love in the body originates. Spirit begins in this pith of flesh that is fundamentally *me*.

I laid bread and cheese out on the stone wall bordering the road. The bread was brown with a thick crust, the cheese a pungent, crumbling farmer's cheese. I drank warm water. Silence pressed against the surface of the mountain. I sat for a long time. Then I took a timed photograph of myself on the wall, knees held within the circle of my arms, my worn green bike resting beside me. When I returned to the states to finish college, this photograph was the one I chose for the yearbook: myself, perched on a pile of rocks, mountains behind me and clouds fleeting overhead. In it I am strong. My face is carved, my legs are well-formed. I am alone but I am not lonely. In my mind I am singing to God the verses from the Song of Songs:

> You are a garden locked up, my sister . . . .
> You are a spring enclosed, a sealed fountain.
> Your plants are an orchard of pomegranates
> With choice fruits, with henna and nard
> Nard and saffron, calamus and cinnamon
> With every kind of incense tree,
> With myrrh and aloes and all the finest spices.
> You are a garden fountain,
> A well of flowing water streaming down from Lebanon.

As in all heartfelt praise, God sings the verses back to me.

In one way my journey ended with the last downhill ride into Bangor, past the slag heaps smeared black in the valleys and through the stacked mining neighborhoods of towns packed closer and closer together. I picked up my mail at the university and read through the month of living that had gone on without me. Adjusting to Japan was difficult for my parents; even the flour was different, so my mother's cookies came out flat. Children followed Marcy down the streets of Accra, begging her to make her puppet monkey sing and swing his arms. From Kyle I heard nothing. I registered for classes. I opened leather-bound books in the library and read Welsh legends with streaks of light from stained glass passing over the pages. I didn't recognize the woman I was now, who knocked on strangers' doors to find company for meals and who became eloquently irate when the Welsh history professor patted her head. When a friend (a woman with black hair down her back and piercing eyes, whom I loved but wasn't quite brave enough to tell) left Bangor for Japan, we stood together on the railway platform surrounded by milling people, and I kissed her. She pressed silver earrings into my hand, long dangling Celtic knots I wore to remember how bound I was to *people*, to family and friends and helpless strangers.

Because I couldn't stop my forward motion, I bought a contour map of the Isle of Anglesey and dodged classes to speed over the country roads. I searched out all the standing stones and cromlechs lit up sideways by the evening sun. I stood in a dove cote eight centuries old and heard the flutter and cooing of pigeons, spotlighted through the sunny opening in the ceiling. Gareth Davis, my lean friend from the bike store, took me to the eastern tip to see the lighthouse. We drank tea together on a beach of perfectly round stones the size of softballs. Seagulls dove with abandon into the waves. Gareth's love for Wales was an adult child's, born and raised by it; mine was a passion, that of a lover. We spent hours on the backs of our bikes crisscrossing the island. Sometimes Gareth stopped to chat with acquaintances picking berries beside the road. I would pause, slightly apart, and listen to the music of their Welsh.

So in a way the journey didn't end at all but simply launched itself back into community—the place all solitary journeys go if they're to have an impact on the world. At the close of a retreat we take that silent space between our self and God which we've finally learned to drink like wine; we take an opening awareness of the sacred and embody it, act it out, live it until it infiltrates every cranny of our day. The kind of love we learn when we're alone leaves nothing untouched. On the Welsh mountain-top I knew God as a woman, not abstractly as the feminist theology texts portrayed, but in a relational way, one that permitted love of my own body and love of other women because women, too, reflect what is divine. This knowing shifted me. What I saw in myself I could see in others. I could see it in the way Gareth looked up at the seagulls, in my Japanese friend tossing her hair, and I could see it on the worn path of memory—the prostrate woman, her neck slightly twisted in the dirt. I once again climbed that trail up the other side of Bangor and found no evidence that she'd been there; I asked around town, but no one had heard of misfortune falling on a single, lonely woman. With humility, I finally understood what happened. God inhabits us. The body I turned my back on and ran from in panic was *my* body, a holy vessel. I ran and ran until I arrived back in its skin.

In the end I was no longer afraid to touch her.

Into the Garden

One of the nice little gusts of wind rushed down the walk, and it was a stronger one than the rest. It was strong enough to wave the branches of the trees, and it was more than strong enough to sway the trailing sprays of untrimmed ivy hanging from the wall. Mary stepped close to the robin, and suddenly the gust of wind swung aside some loose ivy trails, and more suddenly still she jumped towards it and caught it in her hand. This she did because she had seen something under it— a round knob which had been covered by the leaves hanging over it. It was the knob of a door.

For the next three years I was haunted by an image, drawn half from memory and half imagination, of myself standing beside a cliff at the Irish Sea. The slope was absolute vertical, the waves at the bottom a cold green. My soul had been waiting at this steep, grassy edge ever since I left Wales. In the meantime, I had graduated, procured a teaching position at a suburban public school, disregarded my spiritual life and ignored the increasing clarity of my sexual identity. When I stopped to ponder the drop-off into restless water, panic escalated inside of me. I knew that if I were ever to grow again, I'd have to step out from that cliff. I would have to place my weight on the salty air, into the sudden sinking power of gravity. Silence was my small toehold of earth. To leap was to speak a word I had never before spoken.

That image finally pushed me up the steps of an old brick carriage house in the center of the city, where Sue keeps her office. Ivy crawled up the walls of the building and crept around the windows. The idea of a spiritual director made me sick to my stomach; exposing my very private spiritual life to anyone, especially a professional, terrified me. But I felt stymied, and God seemed stagnant. Intuition told me that my spiritual growth depended on sharing that unspoken word. Where else could I disclose it? Before my first appointment, I fidgeted and paced in the waiting room. I took out my grade book and did averages to calm myself. When Sue finally opened the door, offering me a cup of tea and inviting me inside, I rose too quickly and fumbled with my jacket. My posture reminded me of my awkward seventh grade students. I was in my spiritual adolescence; years of reading theology had caused my intellect to outgrow my soul and expose its proverbial ankles and naked wrists. I feared that my word was exposed as well. Under Sue's steady eyes, I feared it and desired it deeply. What my body could say plainly got caught in my throat.

For four months I saw Sue without sharing why I was there. During that time, I realized that the term "spiritual direction" is misleading. It implies a right and a wrong, or that the director points and the client follows. I desired that model for learning; I wanted to sit at a teacher's feet to receive words of wisdom, confident that someone more practiced in prayer and discernment would have the answers to my aching questions. But Sue didn't work that way. Everything you need to know God, she said, you've already been given. She trusted completely (far more so than I did) the direction of the spirit's movement within me. Her role, then, was to provide a container into which I slowly poured the stories of my childhood, adolescence, and my journey in Wales. Together we held them up to the light, looking to see where they were infused with the sacred. Sue's wisdom, I realized, came not from profound insight so much as her ability to listen deeply. It came from her faith that a story unfolding in a place of love is transformative. As I gradually allowed her to be attentive to my journey, with all its dark, crazy and ecstatic moments, I became more attentive as well. Sue's integrity and care held me accountable. I had to come out. Such a safe space demanded it.

Finally, after school one day in the spring, I hit every stoplight for fifteen miles on my commute back to the city. I breathed exhaust from the truck ahead of me. My palms slid with sweat on the steering wheel. The car idled. I had made that trip each school day for three years; most of my colleagues had taught for twenty, and I saw my entire life making this journey—thirty-five minutes spun outward to a place where I hid my identity, thirty-five minutes spun back to my sunny brick apartment, where I collapsed then rose at five the next morning in order to write (a dark, cramped half hour for my real passion) before returning to school. Suddenly my life's limitations were stifling. I rolled down the car window to gasp for breath. I hoisted my skirt above my knees and pinched pantyhose away from my skin. Traffic let up when I reached city limits, but my mind grew more frantic. At the curb beside Sue's carriage house I began to tremble.

I opened my journal to write a swift prayer. My script was uneven. *Sue is an ear and a conduit. In reality, you are the one*

I am coming out to. This, today, is the real confession because you work through people. More than any day, today I need your strength. I opened the car door and climbed out, holding my journal to my chest like a closed parachute.

Inside, the carriage house was thick with silence. I had swallowed the city's noisy frenzy and walked in with it, reeling in panic. My chest was so tight that the twelve stairs to the second floor did me in. I tried to sit still and I tried to breathe. If the focused silence of Sue's space could exist in the middle of the city, surely it could also exist within me.

Sue emerged from her room to welcome me. I folded myself into her loveseat, placing my journal on the cushion beside me. I tried to trust Sue, who sat down in her rocker and placed her hands in her lap. She wore a bright plaid skirt and practical black shoes that made her ankles look old. On the table beside her burned a small candle. The oak outside the window rubbed against the screen. As she had each time I'd come to see her over the past four months, Sue waited for me to begin. The silence choked me. I couldn't bring myself to look her in the face.

There are times when the spiritual direction relationship is primarily symbolic; as long as Sue manifests confidence, receptivity, and grace, it doesn't matter who she is personally. She could be my mother or a teacher or the church. She could be an empty page in my journal, onto which I spill the messiness of my life. She could be God, patient, faithful, challenging me to be equally committed.

But that afternoon, despite what I'd written in my journal, the particulars of who she was mattered terribly. She was Sue, white-haired, lover of red tulips and primroses, climber of Kilimanjaro, fan of T. S. Eliot, a woman whose silence usually comforted me. She was a grandmother twenty years the junior of my grandmother; a clergy-woman in a mainstream church who had handed back her ordination papers because her spirit digressed too far from their confines; someone for whom God was not easy and whose career path was far from rote. I couldn't look her in the face, but her hands were tanned and spotted, skin thinning over knuckles. Her wedding ring was a simple gold band, a bit loose. The way her wrists turned upward made me think how human she was, how capable of judging and rejecting me. I felt her eyes, grey and slightly quizzical behind wire-rimmed glasses, watching the top of my bowed head. More than anything, I wanted her human acceptance.

"I haven't been entirely honest," I finally said to my lap. "I feel like the last four months I've been seeing you have been a farce because I've known all along what direction I need to take." I choked with fear and heat and the word caught in my throat. "I know I won't get anywhere in my relationship with God until I tell the truth about my sexuality."

I stole a peek at Sue. She raised her eyebrows when she saw my eyes, and she waited. "It's like this cliff I've come to on my journey. If I want to continue growing I have to jump." But even as I said it I knew I already had. There was no stopping. "If I want to live with integrity I have to say that sometimes I am drawn to men and sometimes I am drawn to women. I haven't acted on it since I've realized this. But I know my body. I'm bisexual." I gripped my thighs with my hands and pulled at the skin. I wished my limbs and their gestures would speak for themselves without the ugly words. It had taken all of my courage to get this far. If

Sue wanted further explanation, the effort would completely waste me.

But instead of asking what experiences I'd had to prove this, Sue chose a question she is very fond of. "How are you with God about this, Elizabeth?" I looked into her face, which remained even and unchanged. "When did you first come out to God?" Her initial concern was my relationship with the sacred—not for the sake of saving my soul, but for the sustenance of my well-being. Was my God one who would uphold me during these difficult times?

I heard this question in her voice and let go of my defenses. The breath I'd been holding I finally released. I sank back into the loveseat. When I first came out to God was *just now*. Sue sat across from me in the rocker, still steady. The world hadn't collapsed; she wouldn't abandon or condemn or doubt me. Sue the human was capable of containing my truth and moving forward with it. My word could exist outside the walls of my body. I would survive.

In answer to her question, I reached for my journal and turned backward a month's worth of entries to three days I had spent on silent retreat. I had been in New York for Easter, visiting relatives upstate and then driving into the Adirondack mountains for some time alone. Five feet of snow fortressed me inside the cabin; the days were warm and I had no obligations. With an empty page of my journal in front of me, I asked the silence, *What is this being bisexual really about?* The charcoal pencil in my hand began to sketch a stone path bordered by overgrown grass and dandelions. The path ended at an arched door made of knotty oak, swinging on cast-iron hinges. Beside the door was an iron sconce and ivy beginning to unfurl its tendrils. The walls were high but crumbling. A pile of fallen stones grew moss at the foot. Over the wall there were glimpses of life: a lanky rosebush with its petals past their prime, an apple tree, an old weeping willow swaying its sad arms. The door was cracked open. I had sensed some long untouched secret inside. Something about the place was strangely familiar.

Now I turned to this page for Sue, bending back the cover and holding the drawing between us. In the corner margin I had written, with surprise, "It's not a closet after all!" There had been a subtle moment when the garden was unfolding under my pencil that I intuited God's approval, however I might name my sexuality. I hoped Sue would see this in my drawing. The pages trembled in my hands.

"Oh, Elizabeth!" Sue exclaimed. She startled me into looking at her again. Her eyes lit up like a little girl's; I'd never seen her bounce in her chair before. "It's the secret garden! It's beautiful!"

I blushed. My drawing was simple and childish. But Sue was looking beyond the lines. She thought the garden they represented was full of delight.

"Maybe I'm putting too much of myself in this," she added quickly, "because the secret garden has always been a meaningful image to me. But remember? The garden lay dormant until Mary found the key and entered and began digging out weeds. A boy learned to walk there. They tended it until it blossomed and was fruitful. And then the door wasn't locked anymore; people came in and out at will." *The Secret Garden*—I barely remembered the story. I must have read Frances Hodgson Burnett's novel when I was eight years old.

Sue was so excited, I looked at the drawing again. When it first emerged from under my pencil, I had thought perhaps it was a garden of Eden luring me inside. Sexuality was a place of temptation, however beautiful. Now I saw nothing deceptive about the apple tree and nothing threatening about the thorny rose bush. The open door was an invitation. To Sue I said, "It feels like this is about *coming into* rather than coming out. God wants me to come into my truth."

"What was the key?" Sue asked. I vaguely remembered that, in the novel, the garden had been locked for years. "Most of the time finding the key is the hardest part."

I hesitated. What had unlocked this rich image, when for most people a deviant sexual identity was a horror to keep behind closed doors? What had opened the possibility that being drawn to both men and women might be a good thing? The only key I could ever remember finding was hinted at in "Mistress of Her Choice"—an imaginary key that allowed me to play at whatever I wished inside the realm of a story. And so I told Sue how in kindergarten I used to swing over the sand and shimmering heat, pumping my legs, the wind flapping my skirt. If I could reach the height where, leaning back, all I saw was afternoon blue, I believed I would fly up into that sky world. In this fantasy place there were no rules; there I could be the beautiful, magical girl I most desired to be. All I had to do was swing high enough and let go of the chains. That was the key. In my imagination I was tossed into a freewheeling, matriarchal realm. I wore emerald gowns. I rested my head in the lap of the queen, and she stroked my hair gently. Later, I led a pro-democracy movement, ushered the people through worship, and fell in love randomly, without restraint. I was wild and most *me* in my imagination.

My childhood was wrought with spirit, fused through and through with wonder and caring relationships. Somewhere, at some time, I was given permission to use my imagination. The stories I told myself before bed did for me as a child what I believe prayer does for the faithful—they gave me confidence in what the world calls impossible. In them I revised societal rules about love until they were broad enough to encompass the complexity of my experience. I imagined life inside the garden in my last waking moments, I told Sue, and during the day strove to embody those dreams.

"Then they make up your vision," Sue said. I shrunk a bit into the sofa, disconcerted by her extravagant choice of words. The world of childhood fantasy seemed remote and hardly visionary. I had worked hard, in college and in my teaching career, to put distance between what I had dreamt up as a child and my adult self. They seemed mutually exclusive.

But those early stories, spun at night with abandon, taught me to trust that God loves love in all forms. Even into adulthood I carried this rare key, this trust, buried under the soil of my days. Sitting in Sue's office, I determined to enter the garden, where I'd find thorns and fruit and the possibility for much growth. There, I felt sure, God could continue to create me. Through the terrible process of truth-telling, I would again grow in spirit.

For a moment Sue and I sat quietly. The silence between us was electric with my coming out and her active listening. Suddenly I felt exhausted.

I rose to go. Sue did as well, but she paused and caught my eyes with hers. "I feel honored that you've shared this with me, Elizabeth," she said. She regarded me warmly. Behind glasses her eyes were still round. I felt surprised and humbled; in her eyes my word, spoken aloud, had deepened and widened me. I felt fleshed out, three-dimensional for the first time since I could remember. The word bisexual loosened the air in my lungs. I breathed from my abdomen into life and limbs.

As I walked down the carriage house stairs and out to the car, I was struck by a stunning thought that bound inextricably the intricate, passionate workings of my body to my creator: What had pulled me out of the closet was desire for God. I had leapt from the precipice and been upheld by angels.

Digging with a Pointed Stick

She did not know anything about gardening, but the grass seemed so thick in some of the places where the green points were pushing their way through that she thought they did not seem to have room enough to grow. She searched about until she found a rather sharp piece of wood and knelt down and dug and weeded out the weeds and grass until she made nice little clear places around them.

"Now they look as if they could breathe," she said, after she had finished with the first ones.

I spent the summer after coming out to Sue sorting through memories, trying to clear space around each recollection so it might teach me what I most needed to know. This is what I had neglected to do when I returned to the states four years earlier. My reentry had left little time for reflection, as I had a major paper to write and a job to find. The journey begun in Wales I had put on hold for the more pressing, practical matter of teaching. It was the plot-line I'd always assumed my life was supposed to take, and for three years I lived it in a frenzy.

But every once in a while, some event shatters the mundane story we've used to frame our lives and we step over the shards into a truer story, a bigger story, one closer to our heart. Sue, in her lavish way, may call this "vision," but in practice it's not the least bit glamorous. Pieces of sharp narrative are scattered all over. For a while it seems there is no story at all, since there is no consistent context and no ordered timeline. The threshold into a more honest image of self is a dangerous place.

Coming out disrupted my comfortable story. I tried to push aside my expectations of success and security in order to get perspective on who I was and what I wanted. My quest to know God demanded that I take the truth about my sexual identity and move it outward from Sue's safe space into the world. I wanted to tell my family first. For years my friends had respectfully avoided personal pronouns in reference to my potential partners; coming out to them wouldn't be easy but there was less to fear. My family was a great unknown. I desired their acceptance the same way I desired prayer, with an ache to be connected to my life's origin. As my trip to New York at the end of August loomed nearer, the ache grew intense, as did my panic.

I had bad timing. My parents had returned to Tarrytown in June after four animated years in Tokyo, and were struggling with reculturization. Tarrytown and the expectations of their old friends seemed stiflingly small. They had boxes to unpack and my father had a new job to adjust to. Marcy was also back in the states living the vagrant's life, driving a VW bus full of friends down from Homer, Alaska, south to who knew where. Her year of poverty in Africa had made her footloose, rootless, and determined to have few attachments. She sent letters simultaneously to my parents and me, postmarked Chico, California, announcing she was pregnant out of wedlock. The news sent my parents into a tailspin. How would Marcy provide for the child? Who would give her emotional support? What (yes, they were embarrassed to admit it) would the neighbors say? Nothing was happening the way they had expected. When Marcy called a month later from Chama, New Mexico, I could hear fear and the warm secret of motherhood already in her voice. We cried together, half with joy and half grief. For a while I had to withhold even from her my own unexpected baby, my news, which I knew would be equally upsetting. I wanted to tell my parents first, in person.

I took my anxiety to Sue, hoping she could fix it. Sitting across from her I fidgeted with the hem of my skirt. The last thing my family needed was the information that I was bisexual. I was not able to reconcile the rejection in every coming out story I'd ever heard with my parent's practice of unconditional love. I was in agony not knowing what their reaction might be.

She met my angst with an air of exasperation. Her elbows rested on the rocking chair arms and she leaned forward as though straining after something. It was clear the only release valve for my tension was in Tarrytown.

"Have you ever talked about sexual identity with them?" she asked.

"Good heavens, no!" I dug around in my memory and shared that fragmented conversation with my mother in the sunny kitchen, sometime when I was in high school, about our questionable neighbors. "We're surrounded by them," my mother had said. My news, that I was one of "them," would surely turn the world upside-down.

"I can hear my parents asking each other what they did wrong," I said to Sue. "They'll doubt that I know what I'm talking about. I'm their obedient, successful daughter; I'm the oldest. They count on me. And I'm betraying that."

Sue shifted in her rocker. "Would you like a practice run-through?" she asked. "I know what I'd ask my daughter were she to come out bisexual to me."

I nodded. I tried to imagine Sue's daughter, older than me perhaps by ten years, and hoped that at some point she, too, had brought grave disappointment to her family. It's hard to learn from perfection.

"I'd want to know who you've slept with," Sue began. "Are you in any danger? Do you have AIDS?" I began shaking. The questions easiest to answer (no one; no; no) hurt the most. Twenty-six years of being my parents' daughter and they would no longer see me as Elizabeth but rather *this word* with all its connotations. "What are your feelings about monogamous commitment? How do you know you're bisexual? What does bisexual mean?" Sue continued ruthlessly when I didn't answer. The hard questions left me flushed and speechless, my ears ringing. How could I explain?

I was on the sofa across from this barrage, eyes closed and hugging my knees tightly. Not for the first time, I wished I was in a relationship that might justify the torment of telling the truth. If I had a lover beside me, coming out would be less personal. It would then be an explanation of the outward commitments—of my relationship with a man or a woman or of my "lifestyle," whatever that was. Instead, I was turning myself inside out, making the sexuality of a single, celibate person an issue without due cause. I was choosing to say, *Fundamentally, even alone, this is who I am.* It reminded me of my audacious decision at the end of high school to apply only to one college, in the middle of the prairie, where I had never visited. Everyone thought I was crazy for not having first checked it out. But I knew it was where I belonged, just as I knew now, without having been in an intimate relationship with a woman, that the capacity resided inside me.

I imagined my parents receiving my dreadful news. Their hair was grey. The porch light shone too brightly and tree branches brushed against the black outsides of the screens. I took a deep breath, imagining the aftershock of coming out. Slowly the shakeup of Sue's words settled into quiet.

"What is the gift you most want to give your parents?" Sue asked, more gently now.

I kept my eyes closed. "An invitation," I said. "I want them to join me on my journey. None of us should ever be alone like this. I want us to be together through hard times." It occurred to me that this was why I had to tell my parents first, before even my most accepting friends. I couldn't think of any greater gift. Deep down I was gambling on my mother's kuken, with its candied fruit peeking through the white icing, which we delivered to the neighbors anyhow. It was all I had to go on.

"Hold out your hands," Sue said. Above my lap and in my mind's eye, I opened my palms. As though speaking to my parents, Sue asked, "Won't you receive the gift Elizabeth extends to you? Her hands contain the truth." A ripple of excitement (or was it fear?) passed through my limbs. With my word I possessed a bit of potent truth. If Sue could recognize it through all the misconceptions, perhaps my parents would as well.

But later, back in my apartment, I burst into tears, head knocked against the kitchen cupboards. I cried hugging the door frame and then slipped down to the bare wood floor.

Anticipation was too much. This was not a truth I would have chosen. Even if all went well and my coming out dissolved into hugs and tears, as I imagined it might, I still could never return to the seemingly safe walls of the closet. The word *bisexual* was a blazing terror that would transform everything.

A Queer, Pretty Place

"It's this," she said. "It's a secret garden, and I'm the only one in the world who wants it to be alive."

Dickon looked round and round about it, and round and round again.

"Eh!" he almost whispered, "it is a queer, pretty place! It's like as if a body was in a dream."

Mistress Mary always felt that however many years she lived she should never forget that first morning when her garden began to grow.

Riding on Sue's prayers of support, I flew to New York. It was the second week of August; the cicadas were raucous and moths collided against the screen doors of the porch. Behind the house, the Hudson lapped at the railroad tracks, liquid and monstrous. My parents, lit by bright reading lamps, looked up from the couch as I walked toward them. They were expecting me to suggest a game of Scrabble. I held some pages of my writing as though they might shield me from my parents' rejection. If they disapproved of me, they might at least approve of my stories. My breath came in short gasps. In an easy movement, my mother removed her reading glasses and placed them on the coffee table. My father turned to me with the *New York Times* spread across his lap. I avoided their eyes.

"I have something to tell you," I began. It set off warning signals. My father's back stiffened and my mother set aside her book. Their panic scented the air. When I began to speak there was a hidden text more powerful than anything mentioned aloud: *Your daughter is really an alien. All this time she has struggled, unbeknownst to you, with the mystery of her body. Now the mystery has an ugly name. Please believe in what's beautiful underneath.* "For years I've been wondering something about myself," I said. "I wanted to tell you before anyone else. The people I know will uphold and cherish me even after I tell them, so don't worry about me. Sue knows already and is walking through this with me, so I'm not alone. I'm not involved with anyone now. But I'm bisexual. You need to know this." I watched dismay and confusion pass over their faces. My father's smooth brow contorted. My mother was holding her breath. In the shocked aftermath I worked hard to remember what Sue had said, that this was a gift, that I was offering an invitation.

For a while they were silent. Then my mother, her voice cracking, asked, "How do you know for sure?"

I began to cry.

"I don't think *how* she knows is any of our business," my father said. His tone of frustration told me he was at a complete loss.

"I just know," I said through the tears. "It's everything I am. I've been writing about it all summer," and I held out the pages—rough stories of my childhood and adolescence, those lonely weeks in Wales and the numinous moment in Sue's room when I first shared my secret garden. My mother took them from me and put them aside. She began to cry, my announcement unleashing a whole summer of grief. She reached out to me and I joined them both on the couch, a great embrace of tears and fear and regret. The three of us rocked back and forth, crying. "What will this mean for your job?" my father asked. "All this time you've been hurting with this," my mother said. Squeezing me tight, she said, "At least you're safe. At least you have people around to support you." On the ladder of their worries, a bi daughter came after a pregnant one. What was most important was our safety and well-being, and that the family stay connected. Everything else would follow. "We don't know what this means," my mother continued, "and we have a lot of learning to do. But you know we'll always love you." I looked from her wet eyes to my father's, and he nodded in agreement. I sighed. This was what I most wanted.

I left them on the porch with my writing and walked barefooted into the dark neighborhood. My feet scuffed the warm pavement I'd raced and biked and played hopscotch on as a child. I knew these streets by the soles of my feet, from the steep slope of our driveway, along the gutter's curve to the bus stop's hemlock-shaded corner. The street lamps were laden and dimmed with bittersweet. I sent prayers back to my parents, who were in for a long evening. I knew they were passing pages silently between them. If their eyes met, they'd be full of shock: In the instant of my coming out, the story they had hoped to read vanished and *this* was left on their laps instead, this version of their daughter's life filled with hidden longings. With one word, my childhood and adulthood had been rewritten in my parents' eyes. They had believed my growing years were sheltered from sorrow and suddenly knew the truth—that their love hadn't staved off hurt, and that my story, like theirs, was painful.

I walked down to a dead-end street and sat on a guard rail above the railroad tracks, feet cold against the metal. Below me the river seemed sluggish, rolling up to the rocks. I listened to its movement. Coming out was loosening the life in my veins; it was turning the ebb tide back to the flow. I sighed heavily. Had the anxiety of the previous months been due to my lack of faith? Then I remembered something Sue had said—that my foreboding was about more than coming out to my family. I was walking into a whole new framework for existing in the world. Beginning with my first moment of disclosure and cascading outward, what I knew most intimately about myself was transforming all that lay in my path. My fear had been real and warranted. Nothing would remain unchanged. Change was the dynamic touch of God, who, at that moment, was as near as the water. I felt immense gratitude. My blessings were more numerous than the Tappan Zee bridge lights mirrored, shimmering, across the river, or even than the stars.

From mid-August until the first week of school, I did the hard work of coming out. I wrote Marcy a letter and sent it to the small mountain trailer where she was living in New Mexico. Her response was full of excitement—perhaps her big sister was as crazy as she was!—with a mild lack of surprise. Besides, she was six months pregnant; her energy had turned inward where new life was growing.

I traveled to upstate New York to come out to my extended family. My grandmother, hunched in her hand-knit sweater, gave me a hug. I am her eldest daughter's eldest daughter. "I love all my grandchildren equally," she whispered in my ear, "but I love you first." When my aunt asked me to choose between Scrabble and backgammon, I said I could go either way. "Yes," she said. "You're writing a book about that." I was astounded. My family simply went against the grain. No wonder I felt that God loves love in whatever form; I had a family that practiced this daily.

I drove back to Minnesota, stopping in Madison, Wisconsin to come out to my close friend Heather. She jumped up and down at my news; she'd been expecting it for years. "I'm going to stand up in my church and say it," I told her, leaning over my coffee cup. "It's the best place in the world, but I'm still nervous." The small urban congregation where I'd been a member since graduation openly welcomed the queer community. Heather was overjoyed. She grabbed my hand. "I'll be there," she said.

A week later, I rose during a Sunday morning worship service to offer my coming out as a prayer. Heather had traveled five hours by Greyhound in order to hold my hand. It was slippery with sweat; what for so long had been private was careening into the public sphere. During a lull between others' prayers I rose. "For a long time I've been trying to find God within myself, and it's been an extremely difficult journey. It demands being honest with the creation which is me, which reflects God, which is made in God's image." Adrenaline pounded in my head and I clutched the pew. "My journey has taken me to this point, now, where I need to find God in my relationships and in community. So now I need to be honest with *you*, and tell you that I am bisexual, and I need to trust whatever support you might offer. My prayer is one of gratitude, because I would not be where I am on my personal journey if this church's journey had not intersected with mine along the way." From the pulpit that morning the pastor read the day's scripture from Mark, chapter four: Jesus said to them, "Is a lamp brought in to be put under a bushel, or under a bed, and not on a stand? For there is nothing hid, except to be made manifest; nor is anything secret, except to come to light. All who have ears to hear, let them hear."

During coffee hour afterwards, a cadre of middle-aged fathers approached me to shake my hand. They looked half amazed and half embarrassed, the way men behave toward a bride in the reception line. The congregation's lay leader, an elderly woman with a sprightly step, approached me. "I was trying to think who to ask to preach on lay Sunday," she said. "When you stood up and came out, Elizabeth, I knew you should be the one to do it. Will you?" A woman who was in church for the first time after a mastectomy gave me a one-breasted hug. Her prayer had preceded mine in the service and had felt much the same: "More than ever, now," she had said, "my body feels whole." Heather danced circles around me. The seven-year-olds who wrote poetry for me on their bulletins simply continued to do so. For a few weeks afterwards, clumsily revised Hallmark cards of congratulations arrived in the mail. Linnea, a church friend, planned a ritual of recognition for me and all those who had come out. The attention made me feel shy, warm, and profoundly grateful.

There's no such thing as a private coming out. Truth-telling, like prayer, fuses the personal and public realms. It reconnects the fragments within us that are the result of falsification, and joins us to others willing to risk similar positions of integrity. My coming out was not particularly brave, because I had surrounded myself with people who love well, nor was it noble, because political advocacy wearies me. Still, in its innocence and ease it was a witness to change, to the radical work of inclusive ministry, and to the possibilities of incarnation. Living with integrity demands more than simply truth-telling. It asks of us complete and continuous transformation.

I gave birth to life inside the garden the same way Marcy gave birth to Simon, a downy-haired, healthy boy with fingers spread wide to the world. Both births were under circumstances where we'd been taught love was inappropriate but with open hearts we learned otherwise. Over the phone, she told me how gently he moved his arms in his sleep. He learned to roll over, to grasp locks of Marcy's black curls, to smile. We were all moving forward, with wonder, toward the future's potential.

I didn't notice the enormity of the change inside of me until holy week. On Maundy Thursday, the women of my church traditionally gather in an upstairs room to wash one another's feet. I had always been too intimidated to join them. I usually sat in the sanctuary, longing to participate in this simple act that was both ancient and mysterious, desperate to be part of that circle of women. But the idea of putting my naked feet into another's hands—into the hands of a woman kneeling before me—was more than I could bear. I wasn't worthy. The contact was too immediate. I didn't want the responsibility that came with receiving such a gift. If I allowed someone to wash my feet, I'd have to see Christ's presence in that person. If I washed another's feet, I'd have to see Christ in myself. Instead I sat restless in the pew.

On the Maundy Thursday after I came out in church, I climbed with deliberation the back staircase to the youth room. Raucous laughter came through the open door. Inside, there were pillows scattered on the floor, and shoes, and dirty socks. Ten-year-old Sophie had her jeans rolled up to her knees and kicked water into her mother's laughing face when she tickled her feet. The Bible on the makeshift altar, open to the foot-washing passage, was slightly water-stained. There was nothing mystical or threatening about the gathering— only some ordinary people with bread-baking bowls and pitchers of warm water scattered around the youth room, whose walls were badly painted with rainbows. I was greeted by a chorus of welcomes and a pat on an empty chair.

"Let me wash your feet," Linnea said. She pulled over a floor pillow and knelt slowly, gentle with her late-middle-aged knees. I bent over and removed sneakers and socks. Linnea took my left foot in her hands and placed it in the wide-mouthed ceramic mixing bowl. She poured water over it until my heel rested in a warm pool. Then she kneaded my toes, washed between them, splashed water up my ankle and smoothed my arch. She cupped my heel in her hand to lift it out. When both feet were washed, she toweled me dry and rubbed in massage oil, pressing each muscle tense from my day of teaching until it relaxed. I watched her bowed head and listened to the woman beside us playing with her friend's toes: "This little piggy betrayed Christ; this little piggy denied him three times; this little piggy went wee-wee-wee all the way from the tomb . . . ." A chorus of giggles. Linnea placed my feet gently on the floor and stood up to take my place. I felt royal. Then I knelt before her to do the same—to wet her knobby toes, massage the stiff wires of her tendons, cradle her bunions in my palms. Her skin was soft, slightly loosened from the bones. Her feet were my mother's feet, and my grandmother's. Touching her felt full of grace.

Afterwards, carrying my shoes and socks downstairs into the sanctuary, I knew this moment as the consequence of my coming out. Never again would it be as lonely inside, and never as dead. For those who are able to love, places of vulnerability, formed sometimes by choice and sometimes by tragedy, are deep handholds. We reach into one another's weakness for connection and comfort. We touch, humbly, one another's nakedness. God would never again be abstract, a hovering spirit with whom I communed in relished secrecy. God resided in Linnea's outstretched foot, in the possibility that I might enter an intimate relationship, and in the way one truth unfold into another and another until even a place of worship fosters courage. God resided in the newspaper clippings on gay rights issues that my father began sending in the mail. God resided in the moment my mother first disclosed her daughter's sexual identity to a focus group on inclusivity at a regional church conference. I walked up to the altar, my bare, perfumed feet brushing against the carpet. The pastor greeted me by name. From her hands I took juice and bread and ate them on my knees. The bread was dense and grainy. The juice tasted of springtime. It was what I'd always imagined communion to be.

The Fear of Growing Things

"Now," he said . . . "it need not be a secret any more. I dare say it will frighten them nearly into fits."

Every June, a party from my congregation carpools from the Sunday service into downtown Minneapolis for the Pride Parade. The city park is jubilant; thousands mill around in brightly colored T-shirts, carrying water bottles, balloons, condoms, placards, and candy to toss to the crowd. My choice to walk with the church and not with the bi women or with educators is a conscious one. Our banner bears the flame and cross and rainbow flag. The kids who fight over carrying it are sometimes the children of heterosexual couples and sometimes of gay couples. A toddler rides in a stroller with signs on either side announcing, "I'm a baby United Methodist and I have two mommies." Compared with other groups, our rag-tag crew—even the whole section of faith-centered organizations—is quite small. It saddens me that religious institutions historically are the last to risk their necks championing issues of civil rights. Marching is for me a witness to a God who yearns for justice. The dykes on bikes roar up the length of the parade, the politicians throw buttons, the Parents and Friends of Lesbians and Gays cause a thunder of applause, the queens wave their gloved hands from the backs of convertibles, the AIDS hospice workers march solemnly, and we are in the midst of it all, professing that the Creator relishes such diversity.

It is a joyful revolution my congregation is waging. We love the Methodist Church and march against its policy to refuse ordination to "self-avowed practicing homosexuals" (a double-whammy for those of us with multiple preference, who, it seems, aren't worthy of consideration); we protest that the church gives gay couples no choice but to "live in sin." When a church, the body of Christ, loves the bodies of its members, what miracles *can't* happen within its walls? These marching congregations respect their clergy, closeted or not; they bless any union where health and happiness are found and celebrate the identity of all who enter their open doors. God-given truths work their transformation in this way: What is possible for an individual is possible for a community, a congregation, and what is possible for a congregation works change even in the larger institution. I think of Marianne Williamson's words: "We were born to make manifest the Glory of God that is within us. . . . When we let our own light shine, we unconsciously give other people permission to do the same. As we are liberated from our own fear, our presence automatically liberates others." Much of organized religion turns a blind eye to these inclusive congregations marching the city streets. But we're patient. Our witness is a ministry to the church as well as its members. We believe in change.

Radical prayer sheds its illusion of privacy by transforming the public arena; radical faith leaves the charming white-washed walls of a church and breaks into the political realm. More fundamental than any conscious belief about God is the manner in which we manifest what we hold sacred. There is the God we profess and the one we live, day in and day out— the one who determines our practice of the ignominious word, "lifestyle." No matter what our heads or hearts tell us, the God we worship is the one we live. This is where we invest our time, energy and money; this is where our creativity and passion go; this is the object of our love and longing.

During my year of teaching after coming out, I recognized the spiritual geography of my commute: My resources were flung far into the suburbs, away from the heart of the city where my church was, where I was out, where I wrote in fragments of stolen time. What I held sacred in practice was security and an obligation to be socially responsible. I thought this meant holding down a job and making a difference in children's lives.

The silence I kept within the school walls was a submission to the God of conservative suburbia. This God smiled on two-car garages and had boundaries about sexuality as clear as the locked gates of a walled community. There was no forum for deviation. What was not outright sin regarding sexual identity was at least a violation of lunchroom social mores, which dictated that "coming out" unnecessarily exposed privacies. A wedding ring, on the other hand, revealed nothing indiscreet. So much was invested in the constructs of normalcy (the money and energy of lifetimes) that the stakes were high. This God was a moral judge, unwavering in his consistency with a will as clear as night and day.

I walked through the halls of the middle school carrying in me the word which when mouthed would cost me my job or, worse, prohibit me from putting my hand on a child's shoulder. At the beginning of the school year I told my classes that I did not tolerate put-downs, and specifically listed gender, race, religion, height, looks, money, and sexual orientation (that means gay, lesbian, bi, and trans jokes, kids). A week passed and the hate-mail began arriving in my mail slot, cc'ed to the principal. Typed unevenly on flimsy paper, unsigned with no return address, full of misspellings, the contents were so unoriginal they almost made me laugh. Still, my hands shook when I folded the letters back into thirds. On my way to lunch, the principal snatched me into her office. "Remember," she said, "you are always accountable to the parents of your students." For four weeks in a row, a crank caller rang my home at eight o'clock at night and hung up when I answered. Not long afterward, a colleague of mine recommended to a student a novel whose main character had a gay uncle; the student's father stood up during a school board meeting, thrusting the paperback into the superintendent's face, and demanded that the teacher be fired. The superintendent agreed. For a full year, I tried to silence the ticking bomb of my word. I knew precisely how powerful its inevitable explosion would be.

The context of unacceptance makes coming out of the closet political. The Other is in me; that which is most different from who I've assumed I was is who I am. What I wanted to push to the periphery of my identity—this comprehensive, commensurate attraction to one gender or the other, to the creative, contemplative life, to simplicity seeded, picked and composted in the vegetable garden—what is alien to my culture and most frightening to me is *in* me. It is this Other which is threatening. It might mean that the Other is in anyone, or everyone, and at the bottom of things we are each alone and different. It might mean that God is the Ultimate Other rather than the familiar, kindly face that looks an awful lot like our own.

Those of us who embody ambiguity distribute alarm equitably in hetero- and homosexual communities alike. We can't be pinned down. We wreck havoc on the safe assumptions others make for survival. If that single, female seventh grade teacher in room 164—the one binding books with her rowdy classes—if she names herself *bisexual*, then she must be the wild card that's ripping up the moral fabric. The *bisexual* defies everything that's intended to tie this loose construct together. She's an insult to committed, monogamous relationships. She is sexually insatiable. Is there a rule regarding gender-behavior that she doesn't break? More than half of her students come from divorced families; they suffer from shuttling between two households, they lose their homework and toothbrushes and don't know what to give for an address. Surely the *bisexual* bears some blame.

It's easier to condemn those who live outside the rules than to question whether the standards we have for moral behavior, which we hold so dear, are destroying us. Factions in the gay community are no less rigid. The bisexual is a waffler, someone who can't decide and who has an easy out if the social stigmas grow unbearable. She stands in the way of civil rights because popular opinion associates her immorality with the Movement. What difference does it make to anyone if the bisexual is celibate in her singleness, or if she values faithfulness in relationship above sexual freedom? If she understands physical attraction to be toward the individual rather than the gender? What difference does it make that her students love to write poetry and fill notebook after notebook of increasingly articulate prose? What about when she leaves her career for the contemplative life of a Christian faith community? Christian? The contradictions are too many to resolve satisfactorily. She is one of *them*. She is the Other.

Quizzical looks come from every direction. It's generally puzzling that I named myself bisexual while single and uninvolved. Why bother? Isn't the point of coming out to reveal that this woman is your lover? Beneath all appearances, separate from relationships, politics and social mores, is our identity, our fundamental being, a pounding heartbeat. This core is what I bring into the open air. Even after I started dating, it was clear that coming out wasn't so much about luscious, tongue-twisting, diverse intimate moments or justifying a partner's gender as it was bringing to the fore my deepest self. The subtleties of lived potential within bisexuality form my being; only from that solid place of self-knowing do I move into relationship. I claim this identity; it gives name to the physical attraction I experience randomly, recklessly. It is my contribution to diversity on the margins. I claim it and lift it up in gratitude for the expanse of inclusive space within a word.

Even harder is when I claim my Christianity in the queer community. During introductions at a workshop on sexuality and spirituality, I share that I'm a member of an ecumenical Christian community. A transgendered woman in the room stands up and shakes her fist at me. "How dare you say I'm sinful!" she demands. "How dare you say that Christ is the only answer!" I sit at the front of the room, heart sinking. Inside me, I know the real question to be, *How dare I profess a religion that's caused this much hurt?* "Not all Christians believe those things," I respond. "It's possible to be a Christian and accept the validity of other faiths. It's possible to understand sin as that which separates us from what is uplifting, healing, and what leads to justice." After the workshop she and I hash out explanations and are able to touch one another's hands in the end. How could I ever leave the church, whose primary work is to witness to love? Someone must stick around to hold the institution accountable, to heal the wounds it has inflicted, and continue to open and reopen its doors. I name my experience simply, but the repercussions layer themselves until a little word must take on the world.

The story of how we are each embodied spirit is a story of liberation, radical in its theology, political in its transformative power. "Who do you say I am?" Jesus asked the disciples—a deceptively simple question, with horrific consequences. *Name me*, prods the God incarnate. *What you name divine walks among you.* And this is how we become instruments for change. Where God resides is any place that creation is at work and truth is spoken. In the midst of crowds, I claim my body and I claim my God—the Ultimate Other, a creator with equanimity and multifarious taste.

Simon Emanuel

> If there had been one person in that garden who had not known
> through all his or her innermost being that if an egg were taken
> away or hurt the whole world would whirl round and crash
> through space and come to an end—if there had been even one
> who did not feel it and act accordingly there could have been
> no happiness even in that golden springtime air.

At first light this morning I am out in the rain picking bush
beans. They are our mystery beans; in the spring a guest
gave the community an unlabeled jar, and MaryJo and I put
them in the ground on a whim. Now the row is a tangled
mess of vines, still covered with purple blossoms this late in
the season. There must be ten varieties—long green lumpy
pods, white pods with purple striations, green pods with
purple striations, autumnal yellow pods. I pick them on my
knees, the composted soil of the bed sinking under my
weight. I drop them into the big white bulk-peanut-butter
bucket, where they first fall with hollow knocks and then
silently once the bottom is covered with beans and rain. In
the twilight of morning I pick beans and crack open their
shells for the surprises they hold: black and white spotted
cow beans, white beans with maroon stain spilling down

from their umbilical cords, fat green beans. Once indoors, I shuck the wet ones onto pie plates and the dry ones into a big glass jar that we will store on the kitchen shelf all winter long. What doesn't get made into great rolling pots of stew will be planted in the spring.

When I pick beans, it is an exercise in recognizing abundance. I especially relish picking pole beans in the sun, standing on an upturned bucket under the trellis with green light filtering down as though through ocean water. When I brush the leaves with an arm or my back, the dead ones press their sticky palms to my jacket and come off their stems. The canopy is magical—a children's crawl-space, a holy grove. The trellis makes a green A-frame of vibrant life beside and above me.

Beans love to hide, so that at first glance it seems there aren't many. When we planned the menu for the week, I said to Scott, who does most of the cooking, "Oh, there's not many beans. We could steam them to feed a group of four or five." Some days we have crowds on retreat, and at other times a single guest. Out in the garden, though, the half-hour I planned to pick beans stretched into an hour and then two, and there are enough beans to steam for dinner and freeze six gallons. Beans look like stems. They hang behind the trellis supports or right in my face where I see them last. What feeds us is curtained with overgrowth and must be sought out deliberately.

And soon. It is mid-September and already a frost and freeze are in the predictions. Winter sends out early shockwaves in the plains states. MaryJo and I need to get what vegetables are on the vines indoors before we lose them to the sudden cold: great heaps of cucumbers, buckets of green tomatoes, the peppers, the eggplant's purple commas. At least squash, chard and kale can weather the low temperatures. Tonight we will throw old sheets over the flower beds, over drooping foxglove, impatiens with their transparent skins, the lobelia and white phlox and zinnias, in an attempt to hold on to color for another few days. These are the plants MaryJo and I raised from seed five months previously, under grow-lights in the basement. We called them our babies. Winter was raging outdoors while we cheered them up from the soil of their tiny plastic cups. We thinned and transplanted and watered them all summer. Now that it's fall, we're preparing to put them to bed. It feels premature. Minnesota is the land of the short growing season. Everything here dies too soon.

How did I come to be here? The story is half jubilation—finally I am in the garden!—and half grief. Rarely are our reasons uncomplicated. The autumn after coming out I returned to teaching with a sense of dread. Whatever I'd given birth to through the month of August certainly couldn't grow in the public school classroom, under the workload of teaching 135 students to write and read. I had a meager half hour to write myself, between five-thirty and six in the dark morning. The days themselves grew darker until I never saw sunlight except from one to three in the afternoon, angling onto the two back rows of desks. "Can't we close those blinds?" my fifth-hour class asked, squinting at the chalkboard. I felt defeated. I counted the days until vacation when I could hold my new nephew, cuddle and kiss the bundle of creative promise so much more alive than I was.

Through advent I waited for Simon with more anticipation than I'd ever given the Christ child. The stories of their births I listened to with the same amazement. Simon was born at home when my sister was on her knees; a midwife coached her through a birth as humble as Mary's. The story of an incarnate God, born over and over again in a manger and into our hearts, paled in comparison with a life I could touch. Simon was a real baby, a soft-fleshed smiling baby whose milky breath I was waiting to kiss at Christmas. I wanted to cup his tiny head in my hand and feel his fingers wrap tightly around mine. I wanted to hear his hummingbird heartbeat.

Then, two days before winter break, Simon Emanuel fell asleep during his three a.m. feeding at my sister's breast and never woke up again. His tiny lungs stopped taking in air and no one could explain why. As soon as I heard, I stopped breathing as well. Linnea came from church and let me choke on tears against her shoulder.

It was six days before Christmas. Marcy and Simon had been scheduled to fly from New Mexico to New York in two days, but Marcy flew alone instead, immediately, on a bereavement ticket. I left early as well so I could wait with my family for Simon's ashes to arrive. We sat silently that afternoon, watching the sun glint off the river and move across the living room walls. A cardinal hopped the width of the yard. The doorbell rang and the delivery man handed my father a metal box that fit in the palm of his hand. Instead of our soft, breathing baby, *this* had arrived, this sharp-cornered cube which was cold to the touch. Marcy was in hard shock. We clutched one another's bodies because there was nothing else to hold. Christ's birth we celebrated numbly, going through the motions.

I held my breath over the holidays and then, back in Minnesota, I held my breath through an anesthetized month and a half of teaching. In between classes, to keep myself sane, I looked at the cards my students had made for me before they so quickly forgot my loss: "Dear Ms. Andrew, It's sad that your nephew died. I don't understand why things like that happen." My stomach muscles pulled tight. My rib cage felt bruised. He was just a baby.

I kept imagining my sister rolling over early in the morning, the warm south-western sunlight crossing the mattress. I imagined her long black hair tangled as her twenty-three-year-old body turned toward her son. I imagined Simon, curled beside her with no heartbeat. He had long fingers, fine eyelashes, an old-man's face and chubby forearms resting along his cheek. In the one good photograph I have of Simon, he is napping in a willow basket, wrapped in blankets my grandmother knit. The desert sun passes across the floor and over his left cheek. He looks like baby Moses— cradled in the bulrushes, ready to float down the river and grow up to lead God's people out of Egypt. He looks ready for a long journey.

Simon was supposed to live. Children are not meant to stop breathing in the middle of the night, one minute a wriggling bundle of potential and the next, empty bones. Their mothers have pushed everything they love and long for through that opening between one world and another; their families have prayed prayers like knit blankets, wrapping the child even from a distance to keep him warm. Babies are made of hope and flesh. When they die, particularly at Christmas, hope vanishes and flesh becomes untrustworthy. The breath that joins body to spirit is unbearably tenuous. If God resides among us, then God, it seems, also leaves swiftly in the dead of night.

My waiting never ended. I still wait to hold Simon, the empty space between my arms like a bottomless vessel for longing. My mother and I say over and over, "We never got to hold him." Who was he? Who was this baby bearing our blood, who came and left without us ever touching skin to skin? It takes effort to remember that my sister, with her lighthearted smile and firm stomach, was and is and will always be a mother. The presence of her child is as real and incorporeal as Jesus. Simon grows big, learns to color, and, sleeping, sighs somewhere in the silence of our hearts.

At Sue's recommendation, I came to the retreat center for a long weekend that February. I came to cry, because otherwise I didn't think I'd survive to the end of the school year. To teach you have to breathe. I brought with me the Simon-as-Moses photograph and a small candle a friend had given me to burn in his memory. On the drive north, I pictured myself casting off responsibilities and distractions like layers of clothing; I flung them out the car window into snow banks where I abandoned them at sixty miles an hour. By the time I turned up the frozen drive and parked in a grove of pines, all I was left wearing was bare grief. An unusual midwinter thaw was turning the snow soft and dirty. The branches overhead were soggy. Everything was still, moisture suspended in the air. I stood beside my car for a moment to get my bearings: a winding drive to the house, an empty walkway, a dead garden half buried in white. Smoke rose form the stone chimney. When I started down the drive, the sound of grinding snow and gravel under my steps carried through the woods.

I was nervous. Why shouldn't I have been? Even for a few days, a place meant for prayer demands that we shake off other occupying worries and take care of our hearts. The time I'd spent in Sue's room had taught me that sacred spaces demand integrity and the hard work of healing. How fast and furious would my tears come in this strangely silent place? Now that I'd learned to love my body, could I reconcile this love with its inevitable loss? With time to dwell on the immensity of losing my nephew, could I move through sorrow to a place where I might again breathe? It was hard to imagine reconciling Simon's loss. I wasn't sure this was something I wanted.

The front walk was protected by an overhang, with string trailers tied from the deck above down to snow-filled flower boxes. Later, when I asked, I learned that the community grew scarlet runner beans and morning glories here. The strings vibrated when the air stirred. I opened the front door with its handle and thumb latch. Inside, a quiet wrapped itself around me that was unlike any welcome I'd ever known. Silent flames burned within an enclosed fireplace; heat radiated from the brick mantel. An afghan was thrown over the arm of a worn sofa. Coat pegs lining the wall were heavy with winter jackets, and boots stood in muddy puddles along the floor. There was the dry smell of wood smoke and the round resin scent from log walls. A page tacked beside the coat pegs listing my name and room number was decorated with a rainbow drawn in crayon. It made me smile. Every detail here—each sign and afghan and blooming violet—had been attended to, every log laid and stone stacked as an act of prayer. Just as I did when I was a child, I removed my shoes at the door and climbed the stairs in my wool socks. The carpet was worn shag. All along the ledge of the staircase were offerings other guests had left behind: pine cones, smooth pebbles, a bird's nest, the random winding of a vine. This was a place of welcome and comfort. I put my bags down in the room with my name on the door, and I let go.

For three days I mourned the baby I never knew. I hiked through the woods in deep snow; I sat on a log and cried into damp red mittens. I lit the candle, pink and shades of blue like a sunrise or a sunset. On retreat there was space and time to attend to what I had neglected due to the exhausting work of teaching. I curled on the sofa beside the picture windows and wrote the letter I had wanted to write to Simon when he was born. A letter was how my grandfather had welcomed me into the world. When I was old enough to read it, my mother pointed out how there was a secret message in it, reading down the first letter of each line: "Happy Birthday, Beth." To Simon I wrote in black ink in the pages of my journal. I wrote through the page out into the spirit world, which was the only way I knew to reach him.

> Simon, you were born into the sunlight, so I've chosen this bright spot to write to you. This weekend I've been looking for you. I walked along the frozen creek bed and saw the trees the beavers had chewed until they toppled. I looked at the dormant branches with their blood-red tips waiting to explode. All yesterday a chickadee was trying to fly through the window where I was sitting; I went outside to see what she saw, and there was a magnificent reflection of a tree with blue between its branches. That's what I feel like now, trying to reach you—there's only a thin layer of something invisible between us.

I think about you wearing the mint pea sweater—the one with flayed cuffs and the pointy hood—that mommy carried me home from the hospital in. The soft knit that kept me warm as an infant kept you warm. Both of us have lost that infancy. I have no memory of you, just as I have no memory of my infancy, but your death leads me to believe in what I do not know. I am sorry I didn't believe enough when you were alive to participate more in your life, even from a distance. With more imagination, I might have understood then what I do now, that death is one of life's gifts, and by welcoming you into the world I was also welcoming losing you.

You are this mystery, this lost bundle of potential that slipped between our fingers. What is there of you to hold on to? A few photographs, Marcy's drawing of you, the gifts we were going to give you. Everything is us; so little is from you. Still, I love you for your short life, for your pug nose and for the angel-fine hair on your round head. I love you through your death into this life-beyond-death that I'm learning to discover. Now you sing the way dead leaves do, curled leaves which the oak tree holds onto through the winter, rustling when everything else is quiet. Please remain the center and the seed of our family, the way your mother conceived of you.

In the winter sunlight, the air above my candle's flame wavered as though the substance of the atmosphere could be altered slightly. I wrote to Simon believing, as I do, that the page is also made of irresolute material partly of this world and partly of the next, so that what is written travels simultaneously backward and forward in time and is received by ears which don't exist but are how the universe listens. Out the window a scrub oak carved blue from the sky. A cardinal landed in one of the branches, which surprised me because my grandmother says that my grandfather's spirit resides in cardinals and that there's always a flutter of red when she most needs it. The letter in my lap, I felt sure, had wings, too. I sent it out as a prayer into that bright, primary world of child's colors—red and blue and snow and the brilliant sunshine.

I believe the afterlife exists *here*, among the living, where we see only its traces as though from a child's unwashed hands after the finger-painting is done. When Simon died, Julia, the midwife who helped deliver him, went with Marcy to the hospital to see if his organs could be donated. It was too late; he had been dead too long. Julia helped my sister, numb with shock, fill out reams of paperwork. She witnessed how coldly the police interrogated her. Have you had any alcohol in the last twenty-four hours? How is your relationship with the baby's father? When the police gave her a moment "in private" with Simon's body, Julia witnessed how they peered through the venetian blinds to see how she behaved. Afterwards she took Marcy home and bathed her. It comforts me to think of Marcy's tanned body in Julia's hands, the hot water poured and rubbed down her back, her black, wet curls of hair patted dry. Julia's hands have caught thousands of babies just as the babies themselves catch their first breath. I like to think of those hands resonant with new life touching my sister's skin, guiding her out of the water, reminding her to breathe.

Then, in the same way Julia escorted Simon into the world, she attended to Marcy's new birth. Long before it was even possible, there was nothing Marcy had desired more than to become a mother. Simon died, and without warning Marcy was taken with a conviction equally strong to become a midwife. The care surrounding new birth and new death that had been lavished on her, she could administer to others. Grief and her sudden desire fused. Almost immediately she began school with more enthusiasm than she had ever shown. She listened for fetal heartbeats, gave lessons in nutrition, cried rivers of tears, and observed, wide-eyed, how her teachers coaxed, calmed and caught babies from the womb. She is now present to others the way her midwife was present to her, ushering in life and nurturing motherhood. This is Simon's gift to Marcy—this passion for her work which makes her more alive with every childbirth.

As I write, Simon's picture rests beside my lamp. He's asleep in his basket, but he travels with me through every draft and chapter. In a way he *is* like Moses; he has led me out of one place that was suffocating my soul, and into another where there is freedom. On the last day of that February weekend, I joined the retreat center's community in the chapel for worship. My grief was private, but I felt how communal prayer buoyed it up and blessed it. At the noon meal we sat at a round table and laughed at the squirrels trying to tightrope-walk the wire out to the hanging bird feeders. Passing the bread basket around made it feel like family, and the conversation's inclusivity made it clear this was a safe place to be out as a sexual minority. When it was time to leave, I stood in the muddy entryway and the community sang a parting prayer:

159

> May the longtime sun shine upon you,
> all love surround you,
> and the pure light within you
> guide you on your way home.

I pulled the front door closed behind me, clothes bag slung over my shoulder, and thought wistfully, "Wouldn't it be good to call this place home?" The sky was a piercing blue and the snow was trampled in paths down to the creek. From the recesses of my intuition I heard a voice, perhaps Simon's voice, asking, "Why not?" I resolved to return when the garden was alive and the creek overrunning its banks. I resolved to leave my job in order that I might nurture the infant creativity within me, whose lifetime was perhaps very short. I resolved to come out in the fullest sense, not just by calling myself bisexual but by attending to all my dreams, all dimensions of my deepest self. Simon taught me that frost can come quickly. We need to grow and harvest while we can.

In May I returned to the retreat center to volunteer for a weekend. I opened my car door under the pine trees and heard a resounding chorus of peepers. A flush of remembering came over me: All through my childhood the tiny swamp frogs had sung me lullabies. "In your sadness and joy," they had called, "we will sing you to sleep." The repeated, rising pitch brought back to me that moment at the brink of sleep when I was little, when the Hudson River landscape seeped through the window screens and pressed itself into my personhood. *So that is what it was like*, I finally knew, *to be an infant*. I stood for a moment, surrounded by the small-throated psalm. Here was a place where I could become myself. I made plans to move in August.

The sounds here are the sounds of home. Simon Emanuel, God-with-us as an infant, for an instant, has never left me and is more present now than he was when he was alive. Sue says that prayer and love are never wasted, and indeed, the place where I mourned Simon has become the place where I know him. Birth comes fast and furious here. Beans send down their roots in the flower boxes along the front walkway; their tendrils wind up the string trellis and stretch out map-of-the-world leaves. The sun on a clear morning touches this green curtain first thing. The blossoms are scarlet, vulvular, and scattered. Unlike the garden beans, these are easy to spot. They are gangly, seven or eight inches long, thicker than a working man's finger. Some have as many as six knuckles bulging under the green skin. When the pods dry, they shrivel into brown bones.

I pick these, too. They are ornamental beans; they have no use. When I crack open the shell, they are the size of small robin's eggs, brilliant lilac with spatterings of wine and lavender. One is unreal; a jar of them seems too purple to be earthly. We save them for planting time.

Even the new things die. Resurrection, I think, is a different kind of life. It settles into the soil, the alkaline of ashes, the carbon of falling leaves, dead vines, bean shells, the earth composting what it most loves so that nothing strays from its heart for long. We pull the plants; we put the garden to bed. Overhead the chickadees change their song and the oak trees cling to their brown leaves. Death demands keen attention to its details. The beans snap in half. They are steamed and slide on our tongues, unseen seeds that we swallow. This is how close to home resurrection happens— in our mouths, in our stories, in the land we turn over and perpetually mourn.

Thinking Only of the Magic

No one smiled. There were all too much in earnest. Colin's face was not even crossed by a shadow. He was thinking only of the Magic.

"Then I will chant," he said. And he began, looking like a strange boy spirit. "The sun is shining—the sun is shining. That is the Magic. The flowers are growing—the roots are stirring. That is the Magic. Being alive is the Magic—being strong is the Magic. The Magic is in me—the Magic is in me. It's in every one of us .... Magic! Magic! Come and help!"

Here is my prayer:

My palms are crossed with lifelines; my fingertips wrinkle in the dishwater. On my wrist is a curled blue vein that crosses over bone. It's a small bone, and delicate, as though in the wing of a baby bird. It extends up my inner arm until it disappears into the pliant fat of my forearm. The joint it joins there is the remarkable bend of my elbow. When I knead bread, muscles, a woman's muscles, tighten and flex. The bone emerges and falls back under skin to the rhythm of beating dough. My body leans into the growing yeast.

A sacrament is an outward and visible manifestation of an inward and invisible reality. Were you taught, as I was, to reserve the word "sacrament" for acts performed before the altar? Accompanied by robes, holy water, solemn faces, gilt-edged books with ribbon markers, "on the night he was betrayed" or any such utterance? What I didn't know then, standing at the front of the sanctuary in my Sunday best, is that often the very last act to actually be holy is the one we call holy. Sacrament comes not by ritual but by grace. We recognize it whenever something vital connects what's unnamed and moving inside of us to something external, with texture and scent and flavor, like the grains in bread. My inward and invisible reality is a whole singing universe; its outward manifestation, in this prayer, is my body.

The rotary knob of my shoulder is too large for one hand to encompass. From shoulder blade down to collar bone my skin stretches tightly; if ever I draw others' eyes it is to this angled ridge, to the confluence of bone into the hollow pool near my throat. I put two fingers in that place. When I speak, words begin in the depths of my diaphragm; they pass this point of vibrating cartilage and rise to the mouthy cavern where they resound and are released. Breath is vital to voice. Even my skin participates in its sound.

"The potential for a sacramental view of the world of nature as well as of fellow human beings," Joan Timmerman writes, "is increased when the whole of one's environment is viewed as capable of stimulating erotic and creative energy." The erotic links what is solid to what is insubstantial. It is the path love travels from my body to the soft-breasted body I embrace or to the bank of the creek where I lie prostrate, heart to throbbing heart with the earth, or to my own warm breath that rushes down past lungs and abdomen to my toes. That which is spark of spirit is so em-

bedded in creation that energy and matter are indistinguishable: the atom's dual identity.

"You know," Sue said to me once early in my coming out
process, "you don't have to be in a relationship to be a
whole sexual being." I flushed deeply. Between her words I
heard permission to make love to myself. I also heard her
combating the old notion that women are sexless unless
they are sleeping with a man, or even with a woman. With
hindsight, I see that the gift of coming out bisexual while
I was uninvolved was that its ramifications didn't end at a
relationship. Naming my sexual identity opened the possibility of living a complete spectrum of intimacy, with
myself, with others, with those who have died, and with the
natural world and God and my creative work. The erotic
colors our every action and reaction because, of course, the
medium by which we know the world is a body. Only when
we dare to admit it—only "when we begin to live from
within outward," Audre Lorde wrote, "in touch with the
power of the erotic within ourselves, and allowing that
power to inform and illuminate our actions upon the world
around us, then we begin to be responsible to ourselves in
the deepest sense." Then we begin to be responsible to the
God in us.

My bare feet know the reverberation of my voice and
others' voices in the solid ground. My feet sense movement
and send that sensation like a chill up the dry, unshaven skin
of my calves and thighs. In the dark place just out of my
sight, small folds of flesh thicken, moisten, respond to life.
The shiver continues up the tree of my spine, its knots and
branches. It courses the neck's bend, up the hard hollow of
my skull and out my crown. I send love of this corporal ex-

istence from me in ripples of air. I relish its impermanence, which demands that I love fully, now.

The transformative movement of coming out is from the inside outward—reaching into the very center of one's identity where creative energy resides like the gaseous light particles inside a birthing star, and releasing it, a swift chain reaction until everything burns, the core's substance brilliantly exposed to the vastness of space. It's dangerous, the way any sacrament is dangerous. But in one form or another, it's what we're called to do. In Christian terms, we must "begin by embracing the scandal of God's continuing incarnation," as theologian James Nelson writes. The real challenge of the doctrine that God took on flesh in the person of Jesus is in accepting that it's possible a body might contain God. If we believe it's possible, we have to believe it's possible for us. Who can bear that responsibility? Who can bear living without it?

My prayer becomes substantial, a thing with which I make love. When I hold a lover close, belly to belly and breast to breast, I grow aware that the spirit resides in what connects us. When those I love die, I know how surely I will as well, and how what is eternal in me will grieve the aches and delights of this temporary vessel. When I write a story I tremble at the invitation to dabble in the dynamic process of creation. This is the never-ending work of bringing to the surface what is sacred within. I rise and reach as high into the air as I can, stretching grist and bone and connective tissue, stretching eyesight and hindsight, stretching my inner light into the farthest reaches of space. *This is my body.* I offer it up like a loaf of well-baked bread.

On Fire

"When you see a bit of earth you want, take it, child, and make it come alive."

It's an old hypothetical question: What one thing would you grab from your burning house? Don't imagine the rolling flames or smoke choking the hallways; don't imagine the terror of a natural element out of control, ripping through your home. Imagine your possessions, your quilt and piano and the china you inherited from your grandmother, and choose one to carry with you into the aftermath.

I would have taken my journals—seventeen years of bound books, the handwriting inside grown from the wide loops of childhood into an adult slant spaced evenly down the page. I would have taken the intimate record of my prayer life, the night dreams when I was nine, the travelogues, the sketchbooks, those pages embodying my stream-of-conscious story poured out each morning before the sun came up. The love poems I wrote to my seventh grade English teacher. The angst of college years when, unawares, I questioned my sexuality. The recent prose that was slowly breaking in its shoes and growing comfortable, language finding its pace and purpose. "Sometimes the words are so close," Julia Alvarez writes, "I am / more who I am when I'm down on paper / than anywhere else." I had given seventeen years of silent passion to those pages, writing myself into existence, writing myself a voice, writing myself out of the closet, out of the classroom, into a love affair with my creator. Just as I had emerged from the privacy of my journals, they burned. Had I a choice, I would have saved the sheets of paper with which I had entrusted my personhood, from which a new life was being launched.

Don't be fooled. What most of us would choose first is life, and this is what makes the question hypothetical. Fire is hot and fast and we're lucky to make it out with oxygen in our lungs. The most realistic answer I've heard to this question is literary, spoken with the callous flourish of a writer. When asked what of his possessions he would remove from the flames, Jean Cocteau responded, "I would take the fire." The fire—only an aesthetic personality would claim, most likely for its shock value, to want the cause of destruction. In the end, though, the fire is all we *can* take. We run from the blaze with its story caught in our throats. It spreads in us like the burning edge of paper; it colors the past, blinds us for a time, and mars the easy future we'd planned. Later, we tell the story with thanksgiving for the breath it takes to give it voice. This is really our only choice. We can take nothing or we can take the fire. I choose fire, emblem of the spirit, with its horrible gifts.

It was August fourth, a Friday, and I had just spent two weeks in northern Minnesota with writing friends—silent mornings, Lake Superior over my computer's shoulder, afternoons paddling and picking blueberries. My night dreams those weeks were sharp because it was a transition time between teaching and something unknown. In one dream I needed to catch a bus to school and was late. Two of my fellow teachers passed by and I asked for a ride, but both refused. "I can't believe you're not willing," I told them. "It would take so little for you to help me." In another there was a flooded park and a rushing, muddy stream. *I am swimming against the current with powerful, straining strokes*, I wrote in my journal. *A black woman swims beside me. Later she gives me difficult swimming tasks.* I was turning my back on a good, stable job for the sake of my writing and because I wanted to be out about my bisexuality and spirituality. "I want to live from my center," I told Sue. She said, "You want to be intentional about living in alignment with God." Yes, that was it. I couldn't do this while teaching, not with all the radical movement inside of me. The internal changes needed external confirmation.

When I had told my colleagues I was leaving in order to live in an ecumenical faith community for an indeterminate tenure, conversation in the lunchroom grew suddenly awkward. The last day of school, after the kids were gone, I touched the four walls of my classroom, sat down on my stool in the front, and cried. All that summer I vacillated between feeling crazy in my sudden lack of good career judgment, and feeling liberated. When it came time to pack, my belongings became symbolic. I chose what parts of myself I'd keep and what parts I'd leave behind. It made sense to simplify my life then, in the fervor of commitment. Do I carry with me my teaching files? Do I continue to drag around college texts? I sold boxes of books. I gave away clothes and furniture. *What I take with me*, I had decided, *will be only the essentials.* Other than what was practical, those possessions I didn't love I didn't need. My friends moved everything in a caravan of three economy cars and two loads in a pickup, storing it in one bay of the retreat center's large maintenance building. Then I drove north to write for two weeks.

And so on August fourth, the day I returned, I walked into the bustling kitchen with my computer and a backpack full of dirty clothes. It was a time of transition for the retreat center; several members of the community were about to leave and a handful of new volunteers, committed for at least a year's time, were arriving. The dinner we shared was full of energy and anticipation. Bread baskets were passed, tea and coffee poured. The half-dozen guests in the house smiled at our enthusiasm. After dishes we went our separate ways, to pack and unpack. We would move my boxes from the garage to the house in the morning.

I lay on a guest-room bed that evening trying to imagine what the coming year of community living would be like. The humidity was thick. The window was wide open and mosquitoes knocked against the screen. My experience in this place as a guest grieving for Simon, I knew, was different from what it would be like to live here. The steady rise and fall of the cicada chorus sounded like steam rising from the heavy world. Even once darkness had settled, it was too hot to pull a sheet over my sweaty body. How would it feel to do ordinary work, like cooking and cleaning, instead of teaching? What would it be like to pray daily with my coworkers? Will we get along? Who will I become, living in this great log house with a prosperous garden out back? At some point I pulled the stiff sheet up to my chin, but I don't remember falling asleep.

A knock at the door woke me bolt awake. I must have heard the roar outside in my sleep because once I was up it sounded familiar. It was MaryJo—she told me to put on my shoes and bring my car keys; the garage was on fire. I ran out barefoot in my flimsy nightshirt. "Put your shoes on," she insisted. Shoes seemed superfluous, a ridiculous requirement. I slipped on my sneakers, the tongues jammed in front of my toes, and I ran on the crushed heels.

Outdoors the night was blazing. I ran thirty yards from the back door down a grass slope to the maintenance garage. At fifteen yards I entered the circle of unbearable heat. The bay nearest the house was on fire and I could feel the roll of flame tearing into the second bay and the third, where my belongings were stored. At a distance of two car-widths from the garage was my little Honda. I ran to it. The only choice I had, with my back to the fire, the bare skin of my calves prickled with heat, was whether to burn my hands opening the car door or lose my car. Instinct made me turn and run. For a moment I was like a moth near an open flame; the thin cotton of my nightshirt sizzled and I knew that instant when the wings, still untouched by fire, suddenly blaze up. A minute later, I imagine, or a foot nearer the garage and I would have caught, my hair a halo of flame.

I flew from the roar. The flames turned over on themselves through the wood walls from one bay to the next. Outside the heat a clearer-thinking (or was it foolish?) community member grabbed my keys and ran back to crawl through the passenger's side of the car. His car was parked next to mine, away from the fire, but two minutes later, after he pulled mine to safety, his tires blew and the door welded shut. The next morning when I inspected the little Honda for damage, I found the plastic molding around the doors and rear tail light melted like a Salvador Dali painting. The hatchback latch that had been broken was fixed by the heat.

But saving the car, my only possession covered by insurance, was not the choice I would have made. I stood helplessly at the heat's edge as fire lapped up the wooden garage door where my belongings were. I wanted to make a last minute deal: my car for the crate of journals. Or even for the shoe box of computer disks. Or I'd settle for a single love story, written my passionate first year at college. I wanted so little. It was unreasonable not to get it.

Tires of five cars, two parked inside the garage and three outside, exploded like gunshots. Fire reached the two- and five-gallon tanks of gasoline stored at the back of the building, blasted the earth, and billowed up fifty feet past the tops of white pines. Sparks flung even higher, up where the summer stars seemed dull in comparison. The roof beams were burning, the tractor, the wood shop, the next two winter's worth of firewood for heating the house, storm windows, five bicycles, and in the third bay, a great roar of books. The ceiling collapsed. Flames leapt up the surrounding trees and caught the needles of five great white pines. Their limbs were fine black lace. They burned from their tops like living candles.

We huddled outside the kitchen door, sixty feet from the fire. Even there the heat was intense, but not enough to prevent the mosquitoes from biting us ruthlessly, through our nightclothes, through our hair. All there was to do was wait. The guests were evacuated. The windows of the lodge were shut, doors closed, and our collection of household fire extinguishers lay pitifully at our feet. The fire department had been called long before MaryJo woke me up. We sat at the picnic table facing the fire with panic caught in our throats, and we swatted mosquitoes.

I shivered in my thin cotton nightshirt, bare ankles and sneakers. Then, with dry heaving sobs, I realized that my work was burning—a great bonfire of stymied narrative. Seventeen years worth of journals, beginning with the fourth-grade lock and key diary; my only complete copy of "Mistress of Her Choice," fragments of which were caught mid-draft in my computer; my high school thesis on epiphany in *Portrait of an Artist* and my college thesis on contemporary women writers uncovering new ways of doing theology; files full of poems, disks of memoirs, most unpublished, most unread; and my journals, my journals, those records of dreams and despair and delight, the raw material of my life that I was reworking into a book. My book—I raced indoors to my bags to pull out a small plastic box of disks. Four years of effort contained in an object so unattractive. If the house should burn too, this was the only thing that mattered to me. For the next twenty-four hours I kept it on my person.

The entire garage and five surrounding trees were burning by the time the fire trucks arrived. From the phone call soon after the fire began until they turned down the drive was fifteen minutes. The volunteers had come from two towns, both ten miles away, and two of the miles were rutted dirt roads. By then there was nothing to save. They hosed down the trees. They brought the burning under control, meaning they tamed it to twenty-foot flames. One kindly fireman heard that my personal belongings were burning; he waded into the coals and pulled out charred, dripping boxes. He found the loose title page of a book a student had given me; "We are what we remember, and we remember our teachers," she had written. He dragged out one box of un-recognizable journals. Then he picked up melted paperbacks one after the next, asking if I wanted them. Alice Walker? Toni Morrison? Carter Heyward? No. Let them burn. I wanted what was irreplaceable, the record of my life, my history, those clothbound journals that I had trusted to sit on the shelf and remind me of who I was.

Even after the fire department returned with a second truck of water the garage burned wildly. It had been wood-framed, wood-shingled, built by volunteers. Two years worth of firewood doesn't turn to ash overnight. The firemen rec-ommended that we allow it to burn itself out to save us the additional cost of hauling the wreckage. Nothing could be salvaged. The weather report predicted that the wind would rise in the morning. The community took shifts to watch the fire through the night.

But first we gathered in the chapel. Inside, the log walls were match-sticks and I imagined coals smoldering under the floor pillows. We sat in a circle on the rug. We did not light a candle. Our prayers were spoken in shock, through tears, to a God who permitted frightening things to happen. Before heading back to bed where we'd only pretend to sleep, we held one another in a tight group hug. The arms over my shoulders were those of strangers who knew not much more about me than the honest outpouring of my application, and that I'd just lost everything I owned. Together we embraced the hollow of our losses.

Since the fire I've come to believe in omens—not good omens or bad, but just signs that mark a moment, saying *Pay attention here.* At midnight of my first night in a new life, the fire was an omen. Evidence of every moment before that one was erased. Gone was all evidence that I was a teacher, that I'd had my own apartment, that I'd ever traveled, that I had had any past at all. My slate was wiped clean. I was a novice entering a convent, head shaved, possessions removed, clothes replaced by a habit. I was an emptied vessel. Prophetic signs aren't about telling the future so much as instructing how to live in the present. *Live lightly*, the fire said to me. *Live with flaming abandon.*

When you come to a firebreak in a forest, there is a stretch of barren ground before the trees begin again. The intention is that what may destroy the first half of the woods will be prevented from leaping across to the second half, and so the land is divided into pieces for the sake of saving the whole. The growth in that narrow stretch between sections is sacrificed. Sometimes a fire never comes roaring through, and I wonder if it's worth it. Then sometimes it does. The period of shock time—four weeks? eight weeks?—after the fire was my firebreak. The world felt barren and still.

The next evening, Marie, a friend from church, came up from the cities to give me a hug. She brought a bouquet of daisies and a vase to put them in because she knew I no longer had one. We sat in an unlit corner of the common room and talked in low voices. I was numb. Without emotion I tried to list for her what I'd lost. It grew dark. Marie lit a candle, opened a jar of massage oil, and took my feet into her lap. With her thumb she worked the small muscles between bones; she pressed stress from the tendons and smoothed the arches. What felt like dead appendages to me

Marie believed still contained life. A faint smell of pine rose between us. I was exhausted. I fell asleep to her touch.

Dreams haunted everyone in the house—terrifying, communal dreams that we shared with hushed voices around the kitchen table. In the middle of a dinner party a sofa cushion self-ignites. We are outdoors splitting wood and find glowing coals at the centers of the stumps. The root system of the forest is smoldering, fire spreading underground from tree to tree. When thunder cracked the night open, I sprang out of bed shaking, feeling for my shoes. A community member panicked when she drove around a bend in the road and saw the sunset—the trees were on fire! We lived at the edge of disaster. Any instant might consume what we knew or loved and heave us into darkness.

On the third day it started raining. The sky hung low, pressing the humidity against our skin and the walls of our lungs. The bean vines in the garden grew soggy and the rain gauge collected its measurement. Mosquitoes bred by the millions. For the short walk from the house to the fire, I covered every inch of skin—long pants, long sleeves with my hands curled in the cuffs, mosquito netting over my face. The fire burned for fifty-six hours, rain spitting in its belly. Where it had started, the shells of two cars sent wisps of grey smoke skyward. The center of the garage was a smoldering mess of iron beams, sprung garage door springs, melted storm windows; on either end the woodpiles were roaring bonfires. At my storage bay, loose pages of Dr. Seuss were strewn about—a Chopin piano score—a box of hardcovers still burning. My futon's inner fluff was exposed and soaked. I threw a piece of sheet metal onto the coals so I could wade in to my bicycle, that green wonder on whose back I had traversed Wales. It was mangled and corroded, spokes pointing in all directions. The stench of burning rose like a ghost. Later, I scrubbed smoke from my fingernails. I smelled it in my nightshirt when I tossed in bed. For months our food tasted acrid, as though we were eating ash.

When I went downstairs to do laundry, I squirted soap into the washer's gaping mouth and unzipped my backpack of clothes. Two pairs of shorts, a handful of tee-shirts, one sweater. I stood under the bare light bulb of the basement with a dirty sock in each hand. I did not have enough laundry to separate lights from darks. I cried while water filled the washer. Every piece of clothing I owned fit into the space between spinner and the curved, perforated walls.

So few things passed from my previous life to this one that I must pay attention to them. On the fourth day the coals were cool enough to rake through, although I burned the bottom of my sneakers. In the ashes I found a clay sculpture of my big left toe that I made in high school, an iron cross presented to me at Confirmation, an antique pair of scissors and a fistful of corroded quarters. I found a Japanese terra cotta burial horse, given to me by my parents, meant to travel with the dead into the afterlife. Here we were, the horse and I. We'd arrived at this side of midnight scorched a dull black. And that was it. The box of half-burned journals that the fireman rescued was beginning to grow mold outside the kitchen door.

"Actually, you may be lucky," not one but several people told me by way of consolation. "You're not burdened with stuff anymore." Lucky! I was numb with grief. It was true, I decided; objects are nothing, they burn in an instant or melt beyond recognition under the high pressure of heat. The only things of value are what breathes or grows or is capable of telling a story. I had relied on the physical world to be stable and it failed me. When I read and underlined a book, I had counted on it to make up for my vague memory by remaining fixed on the bookshelf, a piece of my experience solidified and trustworthy. When I missed my family or the stunning sweep of the Hudson Valley, I had relied on photographs for comfort. I wrapped myself in my grandmother's afghan when I needed her warmth. And now these things I had loved—my sensuous high school sculptures, the marked and cross-marked map of Wales, a willow basket similar to the one Simon had slept in—these had failed me by burning. Perhaps I was wrong to love these worldly things in the first place. Now I could let them go and refuse to grow attached. I would learn the Christian art of dispossession.

Then the phone began to ring. "What can I bring you?" my friend Carol asked. My mind went blank. I couldn't think of a single thing. "You need underwear and socks," she said. "You need pants and something warm to wear. Do you have a toothbrush?" My friend Joy sent a dress and slip for a wedding I was to participate in the following week. People from church sent scissors, hangers, stationery, kleenex, shampoo, shoes, a laundry basket. Strangers dropped off bags of clothes. I was astounded that others could see these small absences while I floundered in the face of gaping voids. Getting dressed in the morning became a litany—thank you, Carol, for my underwear; Linda for the socks, shirt from Michelle, jeans from an anonymous donor. Suddenly I had become the Bible character, "naked and you clothed me." I felt humbled, thrown upon the world's wide arms. I felt erased by the plain stretch pants and solid tee-shirts that others had chosen for me, the habit for my new, contemplative life. Before the fire I'd worn my personality on my sleeve and let the messages on my shirts boast my politics. Who was I then? I couldn't remember. A pair of underwear was left in the dryer and MaryJo asked if it was mine. I didn't recognize it.

And the books! Someone at church set a box with my name on it beside the food shelf bin, and every Sunday it filled with books—John Jakes, Clive Cussler, books that went from me directly to Good Will. But also a hard cover illustrated copy of *The Secret Garden* given by a nine-year-old; a whole collection of Mary Oliver's poetry, underlined and dog-eared; a wildflower guide that a friend inherited from her mother; blessed books, books that had been loved. Books arrived in the mail as though they were a cure-all, everyone's remedy to my predicament. We're praying for you, they said, but we know a book will work, too.

Others' generosity rubbed on my grief until it let loose. A bicycle. A guitar. A red and white handmade quilt. A desk to write on and a lamp. My mother sent decorative things, a Japanese obi, a small cedar chest, a silver Celtic necklace. Marcy sent a songbook we jointly owned but she had monopolized, and she sent a drawing of a woman with roots in the earth and branches touching heaven. When I cried, I missed the Mexican weave blanket that had always been my crying shawl, but a friend gave me her Danish wool sweater for crying in instead. My initial conviction to detach myself from worldly things by being entirely otherworldly dissolved.

These objects surrounded me with reminders that I was loved. They were signs of family, friendship, community, and, when I didn't know the donor, to God's reckless care for the world. With heaving sobs and sleepless nights, these inanimate things unleashed my love of what I'd lost.

Shortly after the fire, Sue called. A friend of mine had told her what happened. "I'm so sorry, Elizabeth," she said. "I sat in my rocker when I heard, looking around my house, and I tried to imagine losing it all. What do you miss most?" I described for her the large bulletin board that used to hang above my writing desk with a collage of photographs pinned randomly, most of which couldn't be replaced: my self portrait sitting on that stone wall in Wales beside my bike; me and four high school friends in our white graduation robes, all holding red roses; me knitting with my grandmother. Marcy, laughing at her puppet monkey who was dressed in my college sweatshirt. My father, looking up from a phone call with a comical roll of fax paper unfurled across the kitchen floor. My mother's bright nursery-school-teacher photo. They used to hover over me like angels. I missed pictures on the walls and my mother's quilt and Marcy artwork and all the stories that went with them. I told her about the journal I had kept during my bike trip, how I'd sketched the castles and traced maps onto its pages. I missed my books terribly, with their penciled margin notes and authors' signatures, and I missed my journals.

Sue listened patiently, picturing these things as I described them. "You know, Elizabeth," she said when I was done, "I believe you already contain everything that you need to remember." I wasn't sure what she meant. The substance of these objects—their stories, their souls—were contained in me? I pictured the contents of all my files, journals, computer disks and books leaping like wordy spirits out of the flames and impressing themselves in my memory. I would carry these around the same way I carried Simon. I didn't think I could hold it all. "What would you like me to pray for?" Sue asked. I grew tongue-tied. What could I possibly ask of God? "I will pray for presence," she said after I was silent for a time, "and sustenance, and guidance." A few days later a book arrived in the mail. Her inscription was also a prayer: "May each hour be soulful for you. Know that you are loved." With help like Sue's, perhaps I *could* contain what I'd lost.

During that time I had a dream. My mother and I arrived at a restaurant with linen tablecloths. There was a buffet laid out the length of two rooms, lit with candles in pewter holders. Platters of antipasto and lefsa and Thai noodles were piled high. We picked up china plates and filled them as we progressed down the table. I set my plate down between serving dishes for a moment and went back for a croissant. When I returned my plate was missing. I started at the beginning of the table with a clean plate, but then the same thing happened when I put it down to pour my drink. I began to weep with frustration. Why can't I eat? The other diners, wiping their mouths with linen napkins, gathered around me in pity.

For three weeks, the community lived with the blackened hollow of the garage piled beside the house. Insurance company men poked around and came to the door sooty from head to toe, holding pieces of melted car parts in their hands. "There's absolutely no question in my mind," one said. "The hatchback started it. I've seen it in dozens of cases. It happened in an earlier model, and when people complained they slapped a different label on it. Fifteen minutes after you turn the ignition off, or fifteen minutes after turning it on, it sets itself on fire. One elderly man was driving when flames started coming up under the steering column. In this case you can tell because the hatchback is melted from the inside out and the pick-up from the outside in." The vehicles had been parked beside each other in the garage bay.

We sighed with relief: There was a known cause. But four months later, when the fire investigation report was finally released by the insurance company, the same inspector wrote: "The exact cause of the fire is still under investigation. Because the damage to the vehicle was so extensive, it may not be possible to positively determine the exact cause of the fire. It is further the conclusion of this investigator that this fire was of accidental origin and cause." The car was impounded before any further investigations were made. With no evidence and a lukewarm report, any possibility of remuneration was eliminated.

"What happened is immoral," the retreat director told one insurance representative. "The car manufacturer has a moral obligation to inform owners of this defect. It's a case of malicious neglect."

"Lady," he said, "morality has nothing to do with it. Things like this happen all the time. That's why you should buy decent coverage."

Our frustration had no focus. Who was there to be mad at? An automobile conglomerate so enormous that this fire, a minor statistic, didn't register as a concern? The insurance companies, who pointed their fingers at one another until the essential documents were lost? The retreat center, which had me store my personal belongings next to tanks of gasoline and didn't have insurance to cover the losses? Myself, for not having insurance at all? Or God—God?—that creative force we like to call omnipotent to have a place for our blame; did God permit this to happen?

I turned my attention to God. Certainly God gave us free will, the gift of choice which the car company exercised when it neglected to recall a foul starter. Certainly God created the natural element that raged through my life of writing. God was big enough, I decided, to take responsibility for my losses. But did I want to worship this God?

Then I had another dream. I was house-sitting for my parents' suburban tract home, one story with a tiny yard on a newly paved road. It was night, and I hesitated outside of the front porch's circle of light when a kid came up and asked if he could take care of the lawn. I felt uncomfortable and told him no, thank you. He grew aggressive and demanded an explanation. I turned my back on him. Later, he was again on my doorstep. This time I explained: I enjoy doing the yard work myself. He grew irate and tried to block me from reentering the house. His temper and the fact that it was night terrified me. The next day there were people with me in the kitchen; the counters were yellow and sunlight streamed through the open windows. When he came to the door a third time he was ranting, no longer an angry adolescent but a full-grown, dangerous man. Thrashing, he forced his way into the house. Once he was inside, the tension broke. My fear dissolved with the dream and I woke, sitting up, knowing with certainty that this man was God.

When I found myself praying to the warm, mother-God, she'd transform herself into a scrawny teenage boy with clenched fists who thrust his face too close to mine. He forced me to witness his rage. This was a face of God I'd never understood: Jesus raving against the money changers, overturning tables and breaking pigeon cages. I welcomed anger reluctantly, and then joined the tirade. How *dare* large corporations neglect the risks caused and damage done by their faulty products? Their excuse was statistic—not enough occurrences had been reported to warrant a recall. A system where the individual and the small, struggling nonprofit group are singed and silenced so easily by a hulking corporate bureaucracy is unjust. Evil rears its ugly head: the powerful exercise of free will to deny responsibility and, through manipulative disregard, inflict hurt. What happened, I felt certain, went against God's wishes. The garage was not meant to burn; I was not supposed to lose the possessions I loved. Yet in the inevitable, haphazard way that things do, it simply happened.

Finally all five shells of cars were removed. A bulldozer and three dumpsters rolled in to clear the site of debris and lay a new foundation. It was a dripping, grey day. I stood barefoot on the front deck of the house letting the mosquitoes go at my toes. In one sweep, the scoop lifted the rubble of my possessions and heaved it into the dumpster. They evened the surface and spread a layer of sand. Overhead, the ring of scorched pines let their needles drop with the rain. Sap oozed from their scars. I walked down through the wet grass and put my hands into the blackened wounds of their bark. My palms touched a coarse, sticky crust. The trees, too, were weeping with me.

One Sunday the community shared communion together, sitting in a circle in a screened gazebo off in the woods. The heat and humidity were unbearable; we strained for a breath of air, but the woods were still. That morning the psalms spoke directly to me: "Blessed are those who go through the valley of weeping, for they shall make it a place of well-springs." Seven of us clustered in a close circle, knees almost touching, and broke bread for one another. Each of our names was spoken aloud. The words of the sacrament came through a curtain of tears. When the wine hit the back of my throat, my heart leapt. For hours I couldn't stop weeping.

In worship all my barriers fell down. I was an empty plate. I was a flat page waiting to be written on. Who would God create of me now? Already I was no longer who I used to be. There was less of me and more empty space—gift journals with unfilled pages, the large reaching sky over the cornfields of the countryside, the enormous quiet of the retreat center. I shared this with Sue, holding open my hands to show how little was in them. She rose without speaking and left the room, returning with a small sculpture in her palm. She placed it in mine. It was a man hunched over in meditation, the muscles of his back and shoulders pulled tight with effort. He sat cross-legged, his hands resting on his feet and holding his forehead. He wore only a loincloth. I rubbed the smooth teak of his backbone with my thumb. "This is the waiting Buddha," Sue said, reaching out to touch his bent, bald head. "He waited seventeen years for enlightenment."

Seventeen years! His posture and nakedness spoke of waiting. I brought him home and we prayed together for a month. Each day I massaged his spine with my fingers. I sat as he sat, empty and receptive. We presented our blank pages to God.

Only the pieces of my creative work that I was generous enough to share before the fire survived. They arrived in the mail like lost sheep. A paltry collection of poems, a few from my aunt, a few from Sue. From my parents, my college thesis, because the only work I'd ever sent them was academic. I wrote to editors I had worked with and asked for back copies of my professional articles. When I gathered them all together, my collected works fit in one file folder.

I had been selfish and stingy. I thought writing had to reach some state of perfection before other eyes could see it. What I kept secret (because of shame? because of pride?) burned. What I didn't share became an exercise in faith; I had to trust in its memory—trust that somehow I am or the world is different because it once existed. Annie Dillard wrote that "a complete novel in a trunk in the attic is an order added to the sum of the universe's order." I have to believe a burned novel adds its order as well, its sums totaling in the author's every action and reaction. But now, when I remember that writing, it feels like half a prayer, hoped but not spoken, spoken but not sent into the world. Its fruits are limited.

I think of Ezekiel alone in a dry valley of bones. He wanders through this lifelessness, the white wood, the marrow, until the Spirit says, "Prophesy!" and he does, and there is a noise and behold, a rattling, and the bones come together bone to bone. I think of him watching flesh come on those bones like the words of a story filling out its bare idea. He stands in awe at the creation his voice has brought about. The army lays slain across the fields, flesh soaking up the white sun.

These are the bodies of the stories I'd lost. My first grief is that they are gone—the love poems for Merrill, for Mr. Polliche, the memoir I composed in college, my prayers, my journals. My second grief is that they are gone before they'd been breathed upon. "Come from the four winds, O breath, and breathe upon these slain, that they might live," God instructed Ezekiel to say. I had refused to call to the four directions, the places where readers reside (even the small readers, the most important: friends, family), that they might read breath into those lifeless sheets. What I did not share perished. Sue was right; I do carry with me what of my writing was lost, but like flakes of dry skin. Only now have I learned to call on *ruah*, breath, wind, the spirit that makes these bones of words rise upon their feet, an exceedingly great host. Ruah is you who reads them. You are what give them life.

Just before the first snow the great white pines came down. Their tips, their candles, had burned and eventually the five largest would die. Volunteers came to harness their tops and chain-saw through their wide waists. When they fell the earth shuddered. They collapsed across one another where the garage had been, their backs sagging and yellowed needles shattered. We removed the limbs, ran the branches through the shredder, cut the larger logs for firewood, and milled the trunks, forty-eight inches in diameter, at a neighbor's sawmill. I stepped aside and placed my palms on the flat of a stump. It was a dry, clean cut. I counted eighty-five rings. I wanted to wipe the scent of pine into my skin and hair, into the clothes that were not mine, into the walls of my room. The auger came with its great spinning saw and kicked the sawdust of the stumps out behind it until there was only a heap of wood chips and dirt. No evidence of the fire was left on the landscape. Only the root system, tangled beneath the new garage's foundation, remained.

When the new maintenance building went up—a pre-fabricated pole barn, metal—it was hard to remember that corner of the driveway ever being different. We filled the wood shop with donated rotary saws and wrench sets; we hung rakes and hoes alongside the gardening shelves. The season grew cold, so we parked our cars in the garage bays. Storage room in the house was limited, so we stacked boxes of personal belongings in the unused corners. Wounds healed. Guests kept coming on retreat; they called the place a safe, quiet haven. We knew better yet eventually agreed.

Objects, after all, make up the world. They are bits of spirit solidified to remind us of who we are and whom we care for. Loving a thing well is about loving through the material of its make-up to its soul—through the wool afghan to its un-ending warmth, my grandmother's love made tangible. If you love a thing well, it is worth grieving when it is lost. Giving it away becomes doubly generous. After the fire, a care package from Heather, my close friend, included a wood-block print I had given her in college. I had carved four separate blocks to create a layering of colors in the pattern of a quilt; printing took hours. Since then, much to my chagrin, she had hung my art over her mantle. Her pleasure in my amateur work was genuine. This piece, I knew, was her favorite, but she sent it back to me. It hangs on my log wall having been thrice loved—once in creation, once as a gift, and now because it has been returned.

I look around my rooms with awe because everything—desk, rocker, stereo, printer, quilt, photographs, teddy bear, artwork—has been given to me. Which is no different than before the fire, really, except that then my awareness wasn't poignant and biting. My clothes closet is a witness to community. My filled bookshelves are a chorus of prayer. It's odd that God made the world so very worldly. If there is an art to dispossession, it does not include casting off material things with scorn. It involves touching lightly, giving lavishly, and loving spirit wherever it's found. At any instant, all this might burn again—even these words I continue to pull from the invisible world behind the page. Things demand of us an act of faith: that we know what is fleeting and love in it what is eternal. This was God's witness as well when I felt the loose cotton of my nightshirt sizzle at my back and explosions hit the night sky. Everything we are passes in a breath, yet God knows us to be more precious than fine jewels or well-written stories.

"Eventually," Sue told me, "you'll come to see the fire as a crucible. Only what's essential is left." What remains is a third of a journal page from my senior year in college. It sits with me beside my computer as I write, water-stained until ink from one side smeared through to the other. Each time I pick it up the charred edges fall off in flakes. There is the right half of a poem on one side; I can read only the ends of thoughts. One sentence is almost complete: " . . . are treading on holy ground, child." On the other side I recorded complaints of a depression to my friend, and her response. "Heather was the one who caught me," I wrote. "'Elizabeth,' she asked, 'are you writing?'" The fire speaks to me boldly. It mandates that I love what I'm given, grieve what I've lost, and invest all I've got in creating more of it. Tragedy's best gift is the story it writes into your life, not because you then possess something you didn't previously, but because you've become someone more than you were. I *am* the story. Even if my flesh should catch fire and peel away like so many sheaves of paper, even then there is a story. Both creation and cremation, which, without one there is never the other, are chapters. The story is the gold left after refining. I run from the fire with it held tightly in my fist. If it's all that is possible to save, I will save it.

Swinging on the Garden Gate

Inside the garden there were sounds. They were the sounds of running, scuffling feet seeming to chase round and round under the trees, they were strange sounds of lowered suppressed voices—exclamations and smothered, joyous cries . . . And then the moment came, the uncontrollable moment when the sounds forgot to hush themselves. The feet ran faster and faster—they were nearing the garden door—there was quick, strong, young breathing and a wild outbreak of laughing shouts which could not be contained—and the door in the wall was flung open, the sheet of ivy swung back, and a boy burst through it at full speed and, without seeing the outsider, dashed almost into his arms.

The latch to the retreat center's garden gate is a bent nail, driven into the fence post. I turn it in its rusty socket. While I'm in the garden I leave the gate open. Basil and Sage, our barn cats, meander in and out as though this is a novelty, when really they can leap the fence at any time. Basil likes to make himself comfortable precisely where he is most in the way—on the patch of weeds I reach to pull or in the path where I'm steering the wheelbarrow. He rolls over onto his black back once he's gotten my attention and pretends to be thoroughly domesticated. For a while I scratch his belly, but carefully: His claws are razor sharp; I've seen him pounce on a squirrel and pin down its neck. Sage has more self-respect. She is watching from the pump house roof, where she soaks in meager warmth from the October sun.

This afternoon I'm picking the last of the zucchini. Its confident tendrils have shot themselves across the wood-chip path and up the bean poles and tomato plants. When I wade into the morass of zucchini, the palm-open, prickly leaves come up to my thighs. There are still blossoms, lazy yellow sea-urchins lurking in the shadows, some wincing and trailing fleshy vegetables with ever-expanding waist-lines. I carry a paring knife and a bucket. The zucchini, as always, are prolific. What my knees love best is kneeling into the sinking soil of the beds; what my hands love best is twist-ing the bulk of zucchini from the vine and weighing it like a baby. After all the vegetables are picked, I grab hold of that bristly, succulent brain stem where the plant enters the earth. With one yank I bring to ruin the zucchini's reign. The frost would kill it anyway. I shake off the dirt and cut the places where its fingers have tangled themselves in the other veg-etable's business. Then I heap all the tubes of viscous life into the wheelbarrow for composting.

"Live the beauty you love," Rumi tells us; "There are hun-dreds of ways to kneel and kiss the ground." In the garden, though, one way is enough. Until now I've looked for God everywhere except in the dirty cracks of my fingernails. But holiness is so pervasive—I peer into the tips of my fingers caked with soil and imagine mustard seeds taking root there. The garden brings me down again to a child's height, to my knees, where I see grub worms and the intricate pattern of veins on the underside of leaves. The organic lump of flesh in my hands, a baby, a zucchini, takes me back to where I'm open and palpable. My legs ache, my back grows stiff, and I'm in right relation to the earth. It is no longer my mind or heart that is praying, but my body.

Already the plants smell slightly of decay. Leaves heavy with the morning's rain litter the paths. Scott, a community member, emerges from the kitchen to lean against the wire fence and inquire how many of the beans I picked this morning should be processed and how many saved to eat fresh. "Let's steam them for dinner," I suggest. "We could make a garlic butter sauce and serve them with almonds." A guest on retreat wanders up and joins me inside the gate, asking about our yield and what's that long-leafed plant in the herb bed? Sorrel, perennial, its lemon an extra bite in our summer salads. Then she spends a good ten minutes walking up and down the rows, occasionally rubbing foliage between her fingers, sniffing the crushed fragrance.

It's with awe that I roll back on my heels and grow aware that I am harvesting, burying, and praying in a garden with an open gate. When the beans get passed around the table tonight and a guest asks me, for the umpteenth time, how I came to be here and what exactly is the book I am writing, I will tell the truth: I'm looking for embodied spirit, even in this bisexual, single, woman's body, even in the natural world, even in the words on the page. How much of a miracle this is I glimpse only rarely, like now, when I'm head to toe in dirt. The garden is no point of arrival, no place of wisdom where the answers to life's mysteries reside. The gate swings wide and I stand here, open to the possibility of a relationship with a man or with a woman and the blessings of intimacy and commitment; open even to celibacy with its counter-cultural and deeply spiritual gifts; open to both solitude and community, found here, perhaps over years, in the quiet of the woods, or back in the bustle and noise of the city in a radical parish out marching for change. The garden, like a story, is never a place of completion. It is simply where I return again and again to participate in its seasons and to lend my hand at co-creation.

Now that the garden has produced the seeds for planting next year—now that I am in the garden, out about my sexual identity, in between the lines of writing—there are two things that I know. One I learned from experience and one from sharing the experience. God's signature is scrawled in every corner of our lives. When we tell our lives honestly and allow the story to transform us, we help hold the pen.

Once I had a writing teacher who, had I pushed her, could not have told me the difference between free verse and a sonnet. She looked at me askew when I talked about revision, and at one point I had to explain to her the difference between compound and simple sentences. In fact, she taught religion. I came to her with stacks of poems about my sister and how our relationship mirrored my relationship with God. It made me tremble to read her those poems. She was the first out lesbian I ever knew, and she had sharp eyes. When she leaned back in her swivel chair, resting her arm against towering bookshelves, she eyed me as though *I* was the poem and not what was on the page.

Most writing teachers honor the enormous gap between the writer and the manuscript. What winds up on the page is a separate identity from the person who wrote it, and with good reason—writing is inanimate, a construct, a flick of the imagination. It's also much easier to criticize printed matter than to engage the person who gave the matter its shape. It works just as well, we suppose, to manipulate the words until they fit tightly, and to fill in more telling details. Skill is what we most need, then, to write well.

But this professor wasn't interested in skill or writing well. She taught liberation theology, the God-talk of the oppressed and unheard. Instead of looking at the page, she looked steadily at me. "What is your sister like?" she asked. "When do you fight? Why do you laugh? Tell me a sacred moment between you, when you felt connected beyond blood and time." She saw the crumpled sheets in my lap as a spiritual director might, as extensions of my experience as I'd lived it. *Oh*, I thought. *I am the draft. I must be rewritten for these poems to work.* The primary text was *me*; I could revise and fine-tune my life as well as the poem. About theology she taught me that every study of God begins with what we experience and is filtered through the lens of our identity. She gave me the gift of mistaking my poetry for theology.

Which is why I cannot write about my bisexual body being home to spirit without saying that the story is, also. "The Spirit tells our stories to us in the unfolding of our life journeys," Meinrad Craighead, contemporary mystic, writes. What she means is that from our earliest moment of infant awareness, or perhaps even before, a small voice whispers one story (unique, irrefutable) into our ear. It is our life, our primary text. The Spirit tells our stories and we walk through them, groping. But then they are ours. They are written in wrinkles of skin and hard calluses and paper cuts. They enter our stride and spark in the direct gaze of an eye. We each contain a story, a singular, sacred scripture within whose conflicts and climaxes God resides.

I bring my story before Sue the same way I bring my body—awkward at first, stumbling up the carriage house stairs, then easing over the years into its grace. These days, my hands, resting in my lap, are as still as Sue's. I remove my shoes and tuck my feet under my crossed legs on the sofa. In an exaggerated movement, Sue leans over from her rocker to inspect the scuffed loafers I've left on her carpet. "Your shoes look like they have a story to tell," she says playfully. I think perhaps this is how she talks to her granddaughter. "Where have they been today?" I laugh at her question; it seems an irreverent entry into a discussion of my spiritual life. "They've walked the edge of the woods around the retreat center, kicking up leaves," I say. "Into a middle school to teach a writing class, the grocery store, around the sculpture garden. They spent a lot of time pressing the gas pedal. And then up here." I stop and think. "A friend gave them to me after the fire." "Hmm," she responds. We both look for a while at the black hollow where my heel rubs, at the leather rims polished by the wear of my socks. These shoes are as familiar with my feet now as Sue is with my story. She assumed that the answer to my quest to know God—which is, after all, why I come to see her—walks through an ordinary day in these dusty shoes.

When I enter Sue's space, with its Chinese ink and wash painting above the love seat and a small candle burning on the side table; when Sue asks a question, turning her wrist to expose her palm with its deeply cut lifelines, then she becomes like a blank page which is my meeting place with God. Year after year, she takes my story in its draft form, and within the dynamics of a human relationship it is revised and reshaped into a thing more whole, more at peace with its contradictions and divinity. Her listening frames for me, so that I might see it, the expanding universe of my life. This is the work of spiritual direction—storytelling in its most elemental form.

If I had to get at the essence of Sue's theology, it would be this: You never know where God might show up. And God is not static. God is in constant creation, constantly being created. We are not static either; we are in constant creation. Through Sue I've come to believe the spiritual journey is really co-creation throughout every—*every*—moment. Washing dishes. Traversing a mountainside. Grieving lost life. Making love. Marching, waving the banner I believe in. With patience and an ear for what's holy, listening to retreat guests as they unravel to me, in a mirror image of my relationship with Sue, their complicated, ordinary lives. Who we become is shaped by God, and who God becomes is embodied—in the landscape, in our shivering bones, in the story spinning its route onto the open palm of the page. It is, as Margaret Atwood writes, "a naming of the world, a reverse incarnation: the flesh becoming word."

On our long drives across the country when my sister and I were little, we'd play cat's cradle, passing the string contortions back and forth across the black vinyl of the back seat. The string pulled taut between the soft spots of our fingers while beneath us the tires ticked off miles. From New York to California and back, we rode over flatlands and mountains, over miles of blacktop crisscrossing the country. But Marcy and I were more interested in the web we held midair, our five- and seven-year-old fingers sometimes tangled and sometimes graceful. A flick of the wrist, one bent finger, and a thing of beauty and utter uselessness was created between us. When one of us dropped it, the other provided a kick in the thigh. When we invented a new pattern, my mother turned around from the front seat to see. We held strung between us the substance of sisterhood.

It is also the substance of storytelling, or any craft you practice where you participate in your own unmaking. I put forward a pattern, a rough draft, and hold it between my spread palms as though it's a question. Time inserts its fingers and meddles. Or, if not time, then growth or death or the sudden realization of a truth elemental to my identity. The string figure that gets handed back to me is different —burned, knotted, broken open. I work hard to get a grasp on it. I must change. I must come to believe that it is worthwhile to spend years making a seemingly useless thing, a story, with perhaps a bit of beauty in its form and that perhaps speaks a bit for justice. I work under the pretense that I am writing a manuscript, but really God is writing a woman, forming something from nothing, revising, erasing limbs and starting again from scratch. Or we both are writing a relationship, the string passed back and forth also binding us tightly together. Without one or the other of us, not much happens here.

Or God is more concrete even than that. There was a time when I was not yet out of the closet when I'd stand for hours scanning the bookstore shelves for a book that dealt honestly with both sexuality and spirituality, that might reconcile the experience of being bisexual with the Christian faith. If I could find this book, I was convinced, I'd be less lonely and more confident of my sanity. It would be my companion during difficult times. Another person's coming out story could be my map so I wouldn't wander in the dark. With complete, unrelenting desire, I ached for this book.

There was no such book. The gap on the bookshelves gave me a mandate: *Walk into your longing. Write this book.* I had to compose the draft of the manuscript as I lived it, an explorer drawing a map from the middle of the journey, with no perspective. The wilderness of my creative process was also the wilderness of my coming out process—by their nature, both are journeys, frighteningly solitary, that must be groped through before arriving at a place of community. Which is what I was longing for all along.

Throughout the drafting of these pages I reach toward the genesis of this longing. What is in us that aches to grow, that desires connection, that yearns to be uplifted into our common fullness—this I name God. So the meddler in my story may be *you*, who reads this. You dip the fingers of your longing into the pulled-tight strings of the text, and we create it together. What I've thought was lonely work is filled with the company of spirits.

Lay your story down. Lay your story down against the white margin of a page, or lay it with low tones into the listening ears of a friend, or lay it from the pulpit over the startled minds of the congregation. Lay your story down with your magnificent body when you pull your chilly skin between the covers at night. In prayer, lay your borning cry and moment of gravest fear and the sweaty rhythm of sex and your deep love of the landscape you walk on—lay them invisibly over the world. Spread your story on the upturned soil like handfuls of seeds, winter wheat, sown to send nutrients into the earth. There is this soul we all share that needs to be fed. It is aching for your story, for its emotional truths and its flights of fancy, because you must love yourself with leaps and bounds in order to have the courage to tell it. And this is what it aches for most of all.